DEAR

C000015558

A memoir

NINETTE HARTLEY

—— ♛ ——

HORSTEAD BOOKS

First Published May 2021
A Horstead Books Publication
www.horsteadbooks.com

Front cover photograph Will Hartley, will-hartley.com
Book cover design by JD&J Design LLC

Paperback ISBN 9781838421007

Typeset by RefineCatch Limited, www.refinecatch.com
Printed and bound in Great Britain by Clays Ltd, Elcograf S.p.A.

This book is dedicated to all mothers
who have lost a child, at whatever age

My Mummy
She is a sunny morning everywhere
She is a lovely lamb dinner on a big plate
She is a beautiful colourful flowered dress
She is a big soft bed
My Mummy

Thomas Hartley (age 7) June 1991

PROLOGUE

January 13th 2011

Geoff and I walk along the beach. The dog runs ahead but stops when her retractable lead has extended to its limit. I don't bother to reel her back. She's not used to the beach. Most of the time I walk her around our farm, up to the town and back, or let her take herself off, exploring the woods close by. When I do take her to the beach she behaves in an erratic way; barking at nothing and jumping about, being generally annoying. Today she senses that she must be quiet.

I don't cry. I don't laugh. I don't even speak. I hold the lead in one hand and hang onto Geoff's arm with the other as we make slow progress. The sand is naked and wet and even the sharp sea breeze doesn't make my eyes water. It's a Thursday afternoon in January and there's not a soul around. The beach in winter is a sad place: strewn with seaweed, driftwood and many shells of different shapes and sizes. I kick a bit of plastic, I spy several pieces of sea glass but I have no interest in any of it. My mind has taken on a single point of view. Everything I see, hear, taste, smell or touch brings with it only one thought. *He won't see, hear, taste, smell or touch anything, ever again. He'll never meet the dog*

1

now. He loved animals and had been so pleased that we'd saved her. Even though these thoughts go through my head I am, to a certain extent, in denial. I will survive, I know that, but right now the side of the building has been knocked off and it can't be replaced. I need help to shore it up. I lean more heavily into Geoff. Tomorrow we fly from Italy to Porto.

*   *   *

Chapter One

20th November 2020

Dear Tosh,

Ten years ago, today, was the last time we saw each other.

Geoff and I are in the South of France, and we are staying in a small town, a half-hour drive from the Mediterranean. After spending nine years living in Italy, we found the move back to Dorset suited us, but we missed the warmer winters of southern Europe, so a spur of the moment decision brought us here where we've rented a house for six months. This morning, we went out for a walk with Jpeg around the local vineyards. She's enjoying the mild weather too, being an Italian dog. As we strolled down the tracks my thoughts turned back to November 2010.

Emily and Daryl were over from Australia and they generously treated us all to a night at the Hotel du Vin. Emily got some kind of deal; your sister's always good at that. I think she told them she wanted to feature them in an article she was writing about boutique hotels. We were going to celebrate my sixtieth birthday. We all met up in the centre of Bristol; you and Laure were the last to arrive. Later, Laure told me that you had been pacing around the shops, nervous about meeting the family as it would be the first time we'd all been together in a while. It would also be the first time we would see you since you gave up drinking alcohol, and maybe you just felt a bit uncomfortable.

'Sorry we're late Mum. We were looking for a present for you. Here it is. Not wrapped and not very inspiring I'm afraid.' You handed me a small carrier bag, and I looked inside. It was a rather pretty wash bag, black with a floral design. I gave you a big hug. You smelt fresh and clean, and your body was that of a man, no longer my little boy, but I could sense the same vulnerability that I had seen in you on your first day at nursery school.

'Thank you,' I said. 'I don't care what the present is. It's the thought that counts and anyway, seeing you is the best thing.'

It was great to have all my children, apart from Matthew, in the same place. Matthew was in Singapore and hadn't planned to visit England for a while. Joe came over from Cardiff and Wills was living in Bristol.

You and Laure had never stayed in a hotel before: you couldn't afford it. The luxury rooms were huge, with beds the size of tennis courts, walk-through showers, and roll-top baths. The heavy curtains gave the rooms an opulent feel, the dark wooden furniture brought a sense of history to the place. Laure made us all laugh when she told us that you both showered and bathed more times in twenty-four hours than you had in a year. 'Making the most of the facilities Mum,' you said.

We had a family meal together in the hotel dining room that evening. There was that 'elephant in the room' thing going on. I was self-conscious as I drank my white wine. I would try to take a sip when I thought you

4

weren't watching and made sure I drank lots of water. I gave the others at the table a few strong glances when they wanted to 'Order another bottle of wine!' It wasn't that you had an alcohol problem, it was more that your reaction to drinking was not a good one. If the mood was wrong, it became exacerbated when you had a drink. If your mood was okay, then you could have a couple of beers or some wine and all would be well. The fact that you were making the effort not to drink at all was, in my eyes, a massive relief. If you didn't drink anything there was no risk.

I began to chill when I could see you were handling it. A lot of laughter rang around the table that night. Lots of 'piss taking' as families do. The youngest sibling getting the brunt of the humour. 'Good job you were a twin Wills, otherwise you might not be here, 'cos Mum would never have had another one!' you said. You were right of course. I only ever meant to have four children; a nice round number. The consultant said that Wills would be a girl. 'Fraternal twins Mrs Hartley are most often different sexes.' Then he reiterated his words at the birth. After Joe was born, 'And now for the little girl'. But Wills arrived. Emily so wanted a sister, but she ended up with four brothers. I don't remember how long it took her to get used to the idea, but she did, and it's lovely for me that you are all so connected, even if not close in age. That night in 2010 at the hotel in Bristol was magic. I went to bed high on love, and laughter.

Breakfast in the morning was also a noisy family affair; everyone talked at once and a few of us ordered Eggs Benedict to go with our smoked salmon or bacon. 'I pity the poor breakfast chef. Poached eggs with Hollandaise sauce are a bloody nightmare to make,' you said. Then at the end of the meal, you walked over to the kitchen entrance to personally thank the staff, one chef to another.

Emily and Daryl were about to fly off to New York for a holiday, Joe and Wills went back to their respective homes. I travelled down to Exeter with you and stayed the night in the tiny flat you shared with Laure; she had made it so cosy. Everything neat and tidy, the crockery and linen so French. It was a proper little 'love nest' in which you were at home and happy. There were a few post-it type notes pinned up around the place which Laure said you often wrote to her before you left for work. She would usually be the first to leave the house, heading off to study at the university or the library. You knew that she would find them when she came home. Little personal messages, *Sleep well* or *don't forget to…* *I love you*. It was so touching and lovely that they were left up even when they were out of date.

Laure was so good for you; she put up with your mood swings and anxieties. You were lucky she didn't dump you at times but she always saw the best in you. The three of us spent the evening talking and laughing. That night I slept well. I felt closer to both of you when the time came to leave the next day.

You had to work in Cardiff on Monday, and you dropped me in North Devon on your way. I was to stay with a friend before flying back to Italy. You were driving so no need for eye contact. You began to open up and talk to me. Not just general conversation but meaningful stuff; it was something you had rarely done in the past.

'I really like my new counsellor. She's called Wendy. I like her because she doesn't *tell* me what to do. I don't know … she kind of draws stuff out of me. She made me write stuff down, every day. Just for myself. It's good. I think it made me get rid of a lot of anger and also helped me understand myself. She suggested I face people that I have a problem with.'

I felt a tightness in my chest. Is this why you had starting talking to me? Was I about to find out that your mental health issues had been brought on by me?

'Do you have a problem with me?'

You laughed, do you remember? Laughed, smiled, took your hand off the steering wheel for a second and patted my knee. A bit of a role reversal.

'No Mum, I don't have a problem with you. I love you. You've been a good mum. I'm the one that's been difficult. It must have been hard for you at times, especially when Dad became ill with dementia. I know I've done some awful things. But that's not the real me. I'm not proud of the other person I became.'

I asked you about the future and you told me you were thinking of trying to work in an area where you could help people. There's a school for the blind in Exeter and you thought you might volunteer there. You also thought about working with the deaf.

'I really want to try and find a job that I can enjoy. I want to work to help others. I've even been thinking that I could be a counsellor of some kind.' You would have been good at that.

I treasure that trip in the car with you from Exeter to North Devon. We had the opportunity to be alone and you confided in me. I value that conversation and carry it with me, often replaying the scenario in my head. I can't remember if I told you that I loved you. I hope I did.

It took over an hour to get to North Devon and when we arrived at my friend's house you didn't have too much time to spare. I think you made lunch for the three of us before you went on your way. A delicious pasta with a side salad. But, that could be wishful thinking and romanticising on my part. I'm always trying to embellish things.

I love it here in France. I know I won't want to leave at the end of March but we'll have no choice because of Brexit. I can only stay for ninety days in any 180-day period. The referendum in 2016 resulted in a vote to leave the EU and it comes into effect on the 1st January 2021. We couldn't believe the outcome, but there's nothing we can do about it so we just have to get on with it and get our heads around the new rules with the lack of freedom of movement.

I'm sitting in a room which was advertised as a third bedroom, but it's more of a garden room with a day bed on one side. I haven't succumbed to having an afternoon nap on there yet, but I often look longingly at the cushions and the cosy blankets that dress it. On the floor beside me is a black rug, horrendous for showing the dog hairs, but that's where Jpeg chooses to lie, while I write to you; when I look at her I think of you because you never met each other but I know you would have been pals. There are four French doors around the room, giving lots of light, and a desk has been placed in front of one of them. I can sit here and write all my letters to you and look out over the garden. There are a few olive trees dotted about, and I am reminded of Italy and our farm there.

We have only been here since the end of October but already we are known at the bakers and the butchers. Geoff cycles down into town and collects a *boule tranché pour Madame Ninette*. The locals are friendly and we both feel quite at home here. The weather so far has been mild and sunny and we've been able to have coffee and even lunch outside in the garden. A very different

November to the one ten years ago when we were all in Bristol. By the way, I loved that little wash bag and after January 2011 it became a precious item, elevated far beyond its natural station in life.

I'm struggling with the language, my schoolgirl French is not enough, and my brain thinks, 'Foreign language? Must be Italian'. I have to use a translating app all the time. I've kept in touch with Laure so anything really serious and I can message her for help. A lot of things have changed since you left. I'll tell you about them all over the next few weeks, but you should know that Laure married in 2015 and now has a little boy called Antoine. I think you would be happy for her. We certainly are, but it can be painful at times. It wasn't supposed to be like this was it?

I'll write again soon.
Love Mum xxx

SHARDS, A HANDKERCHIEF, AND
PLAYERS CIGARETTES

Cyril Charles Hatch
18th September 1913–28thNovember 1963

I sit on the top stair   hug the wooden
newel post   heavy with beeswax
and peer down into the hallway
                              unnoticed

I can just see the policeman
through a crack in the front door
as he talks to my mother
She leaves with him for the hospital

Despair slinks into our house
silent barriers erected
disbelief   hovers in the corners

My mother brings home his effects:
a leather wallet   full of glass shards
a squashed and broken packet of Players cigarettes
his handkerchief   embroidered with a C
and a small brown comb   with residues
of hair cream   in its teeth

Chapter Two

28th November 2020

Dear Tosh,

Today is the fifty-seventh anniversary of my father's death. Cyril Charles Hatch, what a name! I could never call any of my children Cyril, but I did give Matthew the name Charles as his second name. I don't think I spoke much about my father to you, or to your siblings. I regret that. I was only thirteen when he died, so I never really got to know him as a person. It takes many years to discover everything about a parent or indeed for a parent to know a child as a grown-up. My parents' generation and mine — to a certain extent — still believed that children did not need to know the details of their parents' lives, thoughts, ambitions and certain emotions.

He was an amateur football referee, and a member of the Old Southallians Football Club. Southall was where he met Grandma. They both worked for Ticklers, a food supply firm; he was a sales rep and my mother was a secretary. He and Grandma loved playing tennis. They played in the local club and in the park. I remember watching them on a sunny afternoon through the high wire fence. If I hear that sound of a tennis ball thwacking a racket, I am transported back to my childhood. We spent our summer holidays in Cornwall in a small holiday resort, and my parents entered the tennis tournament every year. My father dressed up in a towelling gown, carried two tennis rackets and a bottle of Robinson's Barley Water. He loved to play the part and pretend he was at Wimbledon. They attended lots of dinner dances, as was the fashion in the 1940s and 50s, and I always looked forward to seeing what gift my mother had been given at the table. Usually a cheap bottle of perfume or a handkerchief or a box of chocolates. Sometimes they used to bring home Kunzle cakes after a works 'do' as they called it. I didn't really like those cakes, but they were all the rage at the time. I forced myself to eat at least one for breakfast when they brought them home.

I don't remember many, if any, serious arguments in the house. My father had a wonderful sense of humour but he also had a strict side to him of which I was a little afraid, although he never lifted his hand to me. A raised voice of instruction was enough to make sure I did as I was told. Once, I remember I had a winning raffle ticket at a primary school event and I got to choose the prize. The choice was an enormous box of chocolates with a picture of some kittens on the front, or a bottle of whisky. I naturally chose the kittens. My father was furious. 'I could have bought you a dozen boxes of chocolates for the price of that whisky!'

We were a happy family. By 1963 Uncle Tony had left home, was married and had two children. Auntie Jean was eighteen and at work but still lived with us. I was the youngest. My father's death came as a massive shock to all of us. It was a Thursday evening, November 28th:

it was dark, windy, and a deluge of rain was falling. My father planned to go to the Conservative Club in West Ruislip and he was waiting for his friend Ray to collect him.

I remember I was sitting on one of the red and grey moquette armchairs, part of the three-piece-suite in our front room. I recall fiddling with the short, fringed edges around the cushions and I was upside down, my legs over the back of the chair, my head hanging over the seat cushion. I liked sitting like that. In fact, I know now that loads of children sit like that on the sofa or armchair, so it was nothing special, but at the time I imagined I'd invented the position. I held a small white paper bag on my tummy. It was filled with chocolate covered toffee nuggets, like little bullets. My father had brought them home for me after work. Always sweets on a Thursday night and I could have them after I'd finished my homework. My father came into the room and put some papers into his oak bureau in the corner. At that time, he worked as a Sales Manager for Liptons Food and travelled around England and Scotland quite a bit. He was a tallish well-built man with dark hair, and a receding hairline. He had a big nose. We called it his 'Roman nose' to which my father always said, 'Yes, it's roamin' all over my face!' Like I said he had a sense of humour, but I can hear you saying that was a pretty lame joke, and I agree. On that night, he tried to grab the packet of sweets and steal them from me, but I was having none of it. I screamed and wouldn't allow him to even take one. We had a bit of a play fight, but I won, and it ended in lots of laughter.

The doorbell rang.

'That's Ray, I'm off now then. Be a good girl and I'll see you in the morning.' He tried one last grab at the sweets, but I held out. He patted me on the head and left the room. Off he went out of the front door, and I never saw him again.

Later that night, when my mother came home from the hospital and told me that he had died instantly in the accident, I felt a heavy guilt. I was so sure that I could have prevented his death. I was convinced that if I could have held him back that evening for a few more minutes or even seconds, it would have delayed the time he left the house. Then he would have avoided the fatal accident. It's rubbish, and a waste of energy; I know that now, but the guilt lived on with me for many years.

Had my father lived, my life would have been so very different. I would not have left school at only fifteen, consequently, I would not have met my first husband and married at only twenty. Maybe I would not have been divorced (if I had married someone else), everything would have been different and from your point of view, you might never have been born. What a shame that would have been.

My father died the week following the assassination of President Kennedy. This event is one of those for which people often ask the question, 'Where were you on the night Kennedy died?' and almost everyone can tell you the answer immediately. I was in a dance class when I heard. I also remember where I was when I heard the news about John Lennon. I was in a hotel in Stoke Mandeville, waiting for an interview to start nursing in the hospital there. Every year, the media mention the anniversary of Kennedy's death, and it always takes me back to that night, just over a week later, when the whole world was still talking about Kennedy; in the papers, on the news, everywhere. Up to that point, Kennedy's death was probably the most significant one that I had experienced. I don't remember any of my grandparents dying as I was too young. Kennedy's had been uppermost in my mind for six days when the horror of my father's accident knocked it into second place.

Our family never blamed Ray for the accident, even though he was charged with dangerous driving and lost his licence. The car in which my father and Ray were travelling, was hit broadside as they turned right into the Conservative Club. My father, being on the passenger side, took the brunt of the impact. It was filthy weather, and a car containing two American forces chaps came racing down the hill from the American Base, where we believed they had been celebrating Thanksgiving. Ray had asked my father if he could see anything coming to which he'd replied, 'No, it's all clear'. The car must have been going very fast but Ray's car was crossing their path so in the eyes of the law, it was his fault.

I think of my father almost every day. I feel sad that he wasn't around to watch me grow up, to give me advice, and to live into old age with Grandma. He would have loved you and all my children. I think he would have been a lovely grandfather but he was only around for my brother's first two and they were very tiny when he died. He may have mellowed in his older years. I will never know, but I can imagine. That's death for you isn't it? Someone leaves a bit early, and you imagine the rest of their lives for them.

I've had to deal with many more deaths over the years: family, close friends, relations. The shock of death, even though sometimes expected, never lessens and I certainly never expected one of my children to go before I did. It's as if we can't accept that death is indeed a part of life. As Woody Allen said, 'I'm not afraid of dying, I just don't want to be there when it happens.' Great line, I wish I'd thought of it.

I'll write again soon.
Lots of love
Mum xx

Chapter Three

30th November 2020

Dear Tosh,

Today would have been your 37th birthday. I try to imagine what your life would be like and it's this: married to Laure, living in France with two children, a boy and a girl. You have become quite a well-known graphic designer, and in your spare time, when you're not looking after the children, you are helping those less fortunate than you; maybe doing some kind of counselling with troubled teenagers. Your easy manner and charm, your well-spoken French with a perfect accent makes you popular with the locals... it's easy to get carried away. Like I said, imagining someone's life when they've left too early is easy. You can give them a smooth and successful run, and a timely death of passing away in their sleep.

Geoff and I are enjoying France, and it would have been a great place to celebrate your birthday. The whole world is in the middle of a pandemic and much of the population is in lockdown, or *confinement* as they call it in France. We have to maintain social distancing — keeping at least a metre apart from others — all restaurants, cafés and bars are closed as are non-essential shops. We are basically stuck in the house. Only allowed out for one hour a day to exercise, including walking the dog, and only one kilometre from home. We can also go out for essential shopping. Bike riding for pleasure is forbidden, and one-kilometre bike rides in a circle would soon be boring, consequently Geoff walks with me and Jpeg every day. When we do go out, we have to carry with us a 'self-certification' document, stating date, the time we left the house and the reason we are out. Masks are compulsory too, whenever you are away from the vicinity of your own home. The UK lockdown is not as severe; people can walk wherever they like but with only one friend. Easing up will be announced on December 2nd but too late for your birthday. The advice and rules change all the time both here and in England.

Coronavirus (Covid-19) has been with us since the beginning of 2020. As a nurse, Joe has been working in the thick of it. Of course! You don't know about Joe qualifying as a nurse. We were very proud of him when he gained a first from Cardiff University. I think you are partly responsible for his success as he worked harder because of what happened to you. To be honest, it made all of us see the benefit of making the most of our time while we have it. Joe is now working on the nursing bank at the Bristol Royal Infirmary on night shifts. He is often on the Covid wards or in Intensive Care. So far, he's remained safe. I think he's pretty good with the protective equipment.

It is so sad that today we did nothing truly significant for your birthday, except that I couldn't get you out of my mind. The weather was cloudy with a damp mist first thing so we only did a short walk with Jpeg. We wore odd socks, which we always do for both your birthday, and your anniversaries (I secretly wear them at other times when I need to think of you). You wore odd socks most of the time so it has become a 'thing' with us. I posted a photo on Facebook of my wiggling feet — one in a green sock with white spots and one red with white swans — I like to make them as odd as possible. I met a young woman through a Facebook group for women living in the area around Pézenas, which is where we are. She's staying here in Caux with her family. She was a theatre producer and is now a TEFL and French Teacher. Her husband is a cellist. They've got three children, a girl of ten, and twin boys of seven. They have relocated to France because of Covid, choosing to settle here for the foreseeable future. Beating the Brexit deadline of 31st December. The family reminded me of our family; energetic, musical and creative. I felt an immediate bond. She saw my post on Facebook, and although we hadn't spoken much about it, she had told me that she'd lost her brother eight years ago. The uncanny part is that the family also wear odd socks on *his* birthday and anniversary because he was known, like you, as an odd sock wearer. She came around this evening just as it was going dark, with a pot containing several cacti, like a mini desert scene. Somebody, the florist I'm guessing, had stuck several small paper flowers in the shape of pompoms on the green bodies of the cacti. The colours are yellow, pink and red.

'I saw this in the shop and it made me think of odd socks so I bought it for you,' she said.

We couldn't embrace: you're not supposed to hug or have contact with others outside your own household because of the virus, but I was so touched by her gift. It's always those who have experienced a similar tragedy that really understand what bereaved families have to live through. Losing a child or sibling when they are still young is so hard to bear, but we all get through it. The support among those who understand, is constant. Her brother will now enter my thoughts when I light a candle and think of you. Because I always think of all the other lost children, especially those whose relatives have become friends of mine.

Every day I think about you and mull over the past but on the day of your birth, I always think back to the early hours of a cold morning in November 1983 when I went into labour. Your dad had not been present at the births of his other children — they didn't allow fathers into the birthing room in the 1940s — so he was extra excited about the whole thing. It was a very frosty morning. I was not at all happy about the pain this time around. I kept repeating, 'I don't like this, I don't like it at all'. Your dad found this highly amusing and always quoted it when recounting the story of your birth to friends or family.

After a slow and treacherous journey, driving through the fog and over the icy roads, it was a relief to arrive at the small maternity hospital in Aylesbury. It wasn't going to be a long labour but it was hard enough, and the gas and air came in very handy. Your dad was so excited and encouraged me all the way. It was quite an experience for a man of seventy. Tears poured down my face and your dad cried with me, you were so beautiful. At least I thought you were, and so did he at the time, but on closer inspection of some photographs years later, I think we were both wearing our rose-coloured spectacles.

We called you Thomas Anthony George; this meant that your initials were TAG. How appropriate in the world of graffiti that turned out to be. Thomas because we loved the name, Anthony after my brother and George because, according to your dad, it was a 'good old English name'. I haven't called you Thomas for a long time. You became Tosh when you were about nine. Do you remember how it began? You had a sweatshirt with the slogan *HELLO TOSH, GOTTA TOSHIBA?* on it. You rarely took it off, and everyone began to call you Tosh. I think a few people still called you Tom: your name badge from work reads, Tom Hartley. I have that badge hanging from the lamp on my writing desk in our house in Dorset. A colleague, who had rescued it from your work place, contacted me via Facebook and sent the badge through; funny how these little things mean so much. I can hold it and know for certain that you held it too. I also have your bag of chef's knives which has Tom Hartley, written on it in indelible ink. I called you Thomas when I was angry with you, but for nearly everyone you just became Tosh. Here's an interesting fact: while out walking with him today, the *Geoff Bates Encyclopedia* informed me that an anagram of Thos, which is the diminutive of the name Thomas is…wait for it…Tosh. An interesting fact, which I did check on the Internet when we got home because we all know how much BS he can come out with. He was correct. Annoyingly!

You were a good baby. I breastfed you for ten months, by which time you were walking, so it seemed right to stop. Matthew was away boarding at a prep school and Emily was at home. She was like a second mother to you, nine years old and she had a real baby to play with. She misses you so much now. It was fun being a mum third time around. We had no financial pressures and I was in a very happy relationship. I could indulge myself, buying trendy baby clothes for you, every conceivable toy that you might need and all the baby paraphernalia I could wish for. Your christening, in the church at Drayton Parslow, Bucks, where we lived at the time, was an indulgent affair. I dressed like Princess Diana and had my hair cut like her too, loads of women did in the eighties. I look back now and wonder what on earth I thought I looked like. I bought you a very expensive white sailor suit shortie. You looked gorgeous, but you had the most horrendous cold. You were a dribbler at the best of times, but on your christening day you went to town and slobbered with aplomb, unaware of the ghastly state of the bib, which I had to sling permanently around your neck. But, you were lovely despite the snot. There was a fusillade of champagne corks, and I'm not exaggerating. Your father, even though he didn't drink for medical reasons, was never one to stint on the alcohol for a good party.

You had many wonderful birthday parties. November is not the ideal time to have a kid's party, especially for boys. Your dad had an expression which was: 'If they can't kick it or eat it they're not interested'. So much easier to have a summer party in the garden with boys. On your first birthday we had a Thomas the Tank Engine cake; I mean, what else could I have done? Family and close friends only. Those baby parties are more for the adults really. You, like most one-year-olds, hadn't got a clue that it was a special day. The second birthday party was with a few more friends and then after that the twins came along — then all birthday parties were organised chaos.

In 2004, it was your twenty-first. You were adamant that you didn't want to celebrate. Your father had died in 2003 and I was living on my own. I forced you to have some kind of 'family' get together and it was a bloody nightmare. I remember being in the garden of my little terraced house in Amersham. At the time, you, Joe and Wills were sharing it with me. You were floundering, not knowing which direction your life should take. Members of the family and some friends, had brought gifts, and given you money, and I felt you had to show some kind of respect. You went through the motions, just to please me, allowing me to throw a barbecue in the garden — even though it was November — and you deigned to speak to people but without much enthusiasm. The icy atmosphere hung around in the house for days afterwards.

They were difficult times. I think it was around this time that you were suffering from a bout of depression and you had your first set of counselling sessions, but you didn't like your counsellor at all. They asked you to express your feelings as a stream of consciousness, and you borrowed my computer to write it.

'I'll do it, but I want you to promise not to read it,' you said, so I didn't. Not at the time. I'm very good at keeping my word and keeping secrets. But when it no longer mattered, I stole a look at the document that was hidden away on my hard drive under a file of miscellaneous items. It was a shock. I was saddened by your angst and the obvious dislike you had for yourself about certain things. Like many young adults you were carrying around a massive burden; mainly about your inability to change the world. You wrote with hate about the appalling things you had read and discovered about the treatment young women went through at the hands of men. Gender mutilation was high on your list. You wrote about people starving, refugees, all the people in the world who were worse off than you. One of the things that upset you was knowing you had come from a privileged background, with a happy childhood, secure within a loving family; this, according to you wasn't fair. *Why me?* you wrote, *why should I have been born lucky?* But even worse than that was the fact that you knew all these dreadful things were going on in the world, and you did nothing about it. You hated yourself for that. It wasn't so much your inability to do anything about it, it was that you were angry that you — *just did nothing*. I wish I had known how you felt at the time, we might have been able to talk about it. But, like most young men, in fact most men, you didn't want to open up to me and admit these innermost feelings. I think you felt enormously guilty that you did nothing, which ended up as a kind of depression. I didn't know any of this at the time. Perhaps, if I had I could have helped you.

Living in the house in Amersham, I always felt as though I was the one lodging with three grown sons rather than vice versa. I found myself hiding in my bedroom in the evenings watching TV while you boys did as you pleased in the rest of the house. I used to shout about the untidiness of the place, and the overflowing rubbish bin. Once, I refused to empty it, as hardly any of it belonged to me, and we played a waiting game to see who would break first and take the rubbish out of the kitchen. I was the one to give in of course, and as I dragged the bin liner out, and filled another with the overflowing crap, expletives rang around the whole place. You all stood around watching me and laughing.

'We wondered how long it would take for you to crack,' said Wills.

You did it on purpose. Horrid boys. I love you all, despite your appalling behaviour at times.

Your twenty-first was the last birthday I think that I celebrated with you. Not long after that, you moved back down to Barnstaple, to a fairly dire flat in the town.

24

I'd lost you then. The scrumptious baby, the wonderful happy toddler, the annoying young teenager; grown and gone. I don't think the love that you had for me when you were a baby ever really changed, it just went into hiding for a while.

After your birth, when they laid you on my chest — I can clearly remember how heavy you felt — the joy I felt during those first few seconds has never left me. The pain of childbirth, the 'I don't like this at all' comments, were swept away, as though they never happened. The smell of your downy head, the miracle of little toes and fingers, a new baby's snuffling and burrowing, searching for the breast. Magic. I know these feelings are common for almost every new mother at every birth, and I can remember these moments for the birth of all my children, and they were all different. You look at your baby in the crib or cot, or when you're feeding them and you cannot imagine ever being cross with them, ever finding fault. They are perfect, with the angelic perfection that only a baby can have. That's my personal experience. A mother loves each child equally, but there is something different about each one. Matthew, my first born, so special for that very reason. It was a difficult birth, the first often is. Emily, my only daughter, popped out without any problems at all. When I got to the hospital at around eight in the morning I said, 'this baby will be born by ten,' and she was. You, Tosh were the first of my second family. Joe and Wills the twins; I remember how privileged it felt to be pregnant with twins, I thought I was so clever. Joe the first one to arrive, special for that reason and Wills the last of my wonderful brood. Each one of my children have a piece of my heart. They are all still in there, but the part of my heart that you occupy is painful and sad.

So many birthdays have come and gone in the last ten

years. On your 29th birthday I wanted to do something crazy and it didn't take me long to decide what it would be. I told the family, and they were all for it. In fact, apart from Matthew who already had one, I think the others were a bit jealous. I don't think Geoff was that keen on the idea but I wasn't going to change my mind. I arranged to meet Joe and Wills in Bristol and we got a cab to the tattoo parlour. It was quite a clean place but the pictures on the walls were a bit scary, Hell's Angels sort of stuff, and there was one guy in there having his whole leg done! My little tattoo seemed nothing by comparison. I had a sample on a piece of paper of your name, Tosh, written in graffiti style. I handed it over to the tattooist and asked him if he could give me a tattoo exactly like it. At first, I was going to have it on my shoulder but Emily said that would be a bit tarty so the family decided the inside of my left wrist would be a good place. I was quite nervous. The guy who did it was mildly amused by my question, 'Will I bleed a lot?' He assured me that not a drop would be spilt. 'I would be a very bad tattooist if I drew blood.'

Honestly, I didn't know if he was joking or not. I laid my arm on the table, palm up and the first thing he did was to make an ink transfer of the design and put it in place on my wrist, just to be sure that it would go in the correct position.

'Yes,' I said. 'That looks great.'

'Right, off we go then.'

It didn't hurt, not really. It was more a burning sensation and whenever it began to get just a tad too hot he stopped. The two parallel lines of the H probably heated up the most. Wills took loads of photos, he always takes loads of photos at every family event but we never get to see that many of them. I don't know what he does with them all. He did post one on social media…a picture of the tattoo with, *My Mum's Got a Tattoo* as the caption. I was so chuffed with it and I am still very proud. I think I'll have to get another one done for your 10th anniversary. I could get it on the other wrist. Maybe *GORF* this time. A copy of your tag.

We have had additions to the family since you left. Emily and Daryl had a little baby girl in April 2013, born in New York; they called her Evie Belle. Emily chose the name for you because you once told her 'life is beautiful, la vie est belle'. I'm sure you said it in French. In July 2016 Emily had another little girl, also born in New York. They named her Orla. You would have been a wonderful uncle.

It was my seventieth birthday in October. Big celebrations had to be curtailed because of the virus. Never mind, I can stay sixty-nine for another year.

Happy Birthday.
I miss you. Love Mum xx

Chapter Four

1st December 2020

Dear Tosh,

The French have lifted the confinement from 1km to 20km. With that in mind, today Geoff and I took the dog in the car and drove to a place called Vailhan where there is a dam, La Barrage des Olivettes. As we drew up we noticed that we were the only people in the car park. I was glad it wasn't crowded. We proceeded to follow the map on my phone and walk up and along the woodland path that would eventually bring us around to the dam. We had looked at the sign in the parking area; you know the sort of thing, an arrow saying *you are here* or in this case *vous êtes ici* and took the suggested 4km walk. But we must have walked the wrong way because we ended up back at the car in about fifteen minutes. You'd never guess that Geoff studied geography at university, his map reading is sometimes very suspect. Our intentions had been good, but instead of a walk we then took a drive. The dog didn't appear to care one way or the other once she'd left her mark in the woods. It was great to escape from the 1km circle around our house, but it was also just a little bit scary, and I was out of my comfort zone.

I am used to it being just me, the dog and Geoff, the three of us at home alone. It made me think back to when you were all younger. A big family with visitors always coming and going and at one point, both your dad and me working. Busy lives we led. I'm still busy now but it's all a lot less chaotic.

There are some things that I might have forgotten to say when I had the chance. We didn't have many long talks or discussions, not just the two of us. There was never time; such a hectic family life, and so much to get through every day. I hope you had a happy childhood. You were certainly a gorgeous baby and very loved by the large extended family. I had gained two step-children, Geoff and Chris Hartley, who were older than me, and six step-grandchildren in the same age group as my children. 'Supergran' they called me.

When I married your dad he was sixty-nine and I was about to be thirty-two. It was a big age difference but it didn't matter to me; your dad looked and behaved as though he were twenty years younger. He was compassionate, kind, thoughtful, intelligent, interesting, happy, youthful. I could go on forever but suffice it to say, he had a very big understanding heart and was a giver. I don't think I talked much to you and the twins about how your dad and I got together. I'm going to begin writing about that now. It won't take long. I know you're not an avid reader but at the same time I think you'd like to know everything.

When I left my first husband I went to stay with Grandma who was living in Weston Super Mare. Matthew and Emily were only six and four at the time. It was a difficult time for me, and for them, but I really needed to get away from their father. As things worked out, I managed to get into a council maisonette on the

Bourneville Estate not far from the sea front at WSM. I was independent but spent a lot of time seeing Grandma and she was a big help with babysitting when I was at work. I began training as a nurse at the local hospital.

Grandma, my dad, your dad and his late wife Hazel, had been friends since the war. Your dad met my dad in the navy when they signed up for service near the beginning of WW2. The surnames Hartley and Hatch must have come up on the mailing list at the same time. Hazel died from cancer in the 1970s and as you know, my dad died in 1963. Grandma and your dad continued with their friendship. I think some people thought they would get together but Grandma said she only liked him 'platonically'. Your dad often used to visit Grandma on his way down from Northwood in Middlesex to Dittisham in Devon where he had a holiday home. I was quite happy in my little council maisonette and one evening your dad arranged to take me and Grandma out to dinner. He did that a few times and then he started just taking me out to dinner and bringing treats for Matthew and Emily. It all grew from there. Your dad never put any pressure on me to be with him; even when he bought me a little house in Buckinghamshire, it was, 'without ties'. He was a truly remarkable man and I think you inherited many of his traits. Your dad and I were married in October 1982. It poured with rain; people say it's lucky if it rains on your wedding day, and perhaps they're right, as we did have twenty-one years together.

We thought it would be a good idea to have a baby. It would complete our family unit and there would be a little brother or sister for Matthew and Emily. The fact of your dad's age never bothered us. I know a lot of people were shocked by the thirty-seven-year age gap but they were even more shocked when I became pregnant.

Perhaps they thought that your dad was too old to father children — I'm not going to go into intimate details with you, but let's just say there were no problems in that area!

According to Geoff and Chris, he was less strict as a father the second time around. He let you get away with a great deal when you were little whereas they had a much firmer set of rules to follow. I didn't expect him to be a completely 'hands-on' dad but he often surprised me with his inventiveness if he had to be in charge of you or the twins for any length of time. I remember once, I had to go off somewhere and I must have taken you with me because I left your dad with the twins for a couple of hours one afternoon. When I got home, he had moved around the sofas and chairs in the living room to make a kind of corral to keep Joe and Wills from crawling off. He was sitting comfortably in a chair reading the paper and as he finished each page he threw it onto the floor. The twins took great delight in tearing it up or pushing it around the carpet. Their faces and hands were covered in newsprint.

'What on earth are you letting them do that for? Look at the state of them.' I wasn't exactly angry, more amused.

'Well. It kept them occupied and I didn't have to keep chasing around for them.'

We had a good laugh about it and then I gathered the dirty little boys in my arms and took them off for a long bath.

Ah, memories Tosh. It's lovely to look back and share some of this with you.

Miss you loads,
Love Mum xx

Chapter Five

2nd December 2020

Dear Tosh,

I walked with my odd sock friend today. I think we may have broken the rules because I'm pretty sure we can only exercise with members of our own household. We didn't see anyone else and the police weren't patrolling the vineyards, so we got away with it. When I got home, I began to think about when you were a teenager. What fun those years were — not. I think that was when your demons began, and when your interest in graffiti morphed from casual interest to obsession. Now is the time for me to say I'm sorry. I'm sorry that I was so involved in running my dancing school, looking after your dad, and other stuff, that I didn't notice the bad things that were happening to my children. It's not an excuse, it's just me analysing my life as a mother. Matthew and Emily were away by this time, both living in Australia; they were adults. I think the first mistake we made with you was taking you away from West Buckland School when you were fourteen. When we moved to North Devon in 1989, we bought Elwell House from the school and it was perfect; a beautiful Victorian mansion set in several acres next door to a good school for Emily to attend immediately and for you and the twins to go to when you were older. Matthew by this time had left home. Unfortunately, after a few years, we couldn't afford to keep you there, that was the problem. It's only now that I appreciate the trauma we put you through. Joe and Wills both went straight to the comprehensive school from West Buckland Prep. They also had each other and a few other friends from their old primary school. You had attended the prep department at West Buckland School from year six I think, and then on to the upper school. You were in year nine when financial problems set in; a result of the massive recession of the eighties. Sending you to the local comp from WBS was a big mistake. You put up with a lot of stick, and bullying which I believe drew you towards the groups with less than desirable members. Or am I making excuses?

It wasn't just your teenage years, it was the build up from when you were eleven to probably fourteen when I perhaps made a few wrong decisions. Apart from running the dancing school, I was also publishing a magazine for young dancers. I had made you go to dancing when you were little, you took modern and tap lessons, and you excelled at it. You were a heartthrob to the girls at the school and they all loved you. You were good at ballet too, but I didn't make you do that for long. What I did make you do — and you never actually complained about it — was to get you to model for the front cover of the first issue of *Youngdancer Magazine*. You looked fabulous. I still have a copy, which I get out sometimes and gaze at your face and eyes, trying to find what was behind them. Did you really hate it or was it peer pressure from others that meant you had to make it appear that you were only doing it under duress?

Your greatest hit at the dance school was when you played the crocodile in Peter Pan. The costume was fantastic, and you performed brilliantly on roller skates. One of the artistic parents made the stunning head from papier-maché I'm guessing. It was so impressive. We dyed a couple of sheets green and painted them to look like crocodile scales to make the body, and the magnificent tail followed you around the stage with a sinister swing. I have a DVD of the show and I sometimes put it on for Evie and Orla to watch; they absolutely love it. 'Is that Uncle Tosh? Is he coming on again?' They sit glued to the TV screen. You were a very scary crocodile.

When you changed to South Molton School you remained friends with Simon Banbury, your friend from West Buckland school who, having spent many a weekend at Elwell House, then continued to spend the weekends at our new place when we moved to Duke Street, South Molton. You, Simon and a couple of other mates up in the top room of our enormous house. You were thirteen when we moved there and fourteen at the end of that year. You were well into your skating and skateboarding then, and both trying to be hip-hop DJs. One night, I drove you all the way to Newquay so that you could take part in a DJ open session. You panicked all the way in the car, about what you were going to play. I had no idea about the scratching and mixing that you did; how it worked or what music you played. I know you spent hours practising in your room. You were influenced by Emily who was a drum and bass DJ in Australia — DJ Emme. I haven't a clue what drum and bass was and I haven't a clue what it was that you played. I watched you spinning the records, listening to them both and switching from one to the other, doing that whacky hand movement on the disc to make it screech. Not what I would call music. But, you were 'very good at it', according to Emily. We arrived home well after midnight from the Newquay trip and found a friend of mine waiting for us. Wills had to call her because your dad had fallen over and he and Joe didn't know how to deal with it. It's very hard to get an old person up on their feet when they have dementia because their brain often can't locate the limbs in order for them to move in the correct way. It was the beginning of your father's decline. Dementia happens slowly, so that at the start it's hardly noticeable. We just thought he was getting a bit old and forgetful, but it was much more than that.

You worked at the restaurant next door as a pot washer. The chef, who was also the owner was a tough boss. He'd worked as a chef in the navy and was a bit scary. Whenever we went there for a meal, he would lean over my shoulder and look at my plate, which sometimes had remnants of potato or meat left on it. I waited for him to say something like: 'Aren't you going to finish that? Do you know how long I slaved over that in the galley? Next time you'll get ten lashes'. The food was good though, and according to him he could cook the best steak in the county. 'I cook the best bloody steak in Devon. No doubt about it'. He would laugh and roll up his sleeves to show his vast sailor tattoos. I shouldn't be mean, we had some good food there and he put on a wonderful spread for your dad's wake after the church service.

You and Simon discovered growing up together. Hanging out with each other trying to get served beer, when you were under age. Trying to be cool in front of girls and smoking the odd joint or two. I expect you felt like a couple of revolutionary comrades but when it came down to it you were just a couple of normal, naughty teenage boys finding your way.

I was too preoccupied with trying to make ends meet financially, looking after your Dad who was deteriorating pretty quickly with dementia, and also dealing with Grandma's care after she had a stroke in 1998 when you were twelve. I managed to move her from Weston to South Molton and settle her in a care home. Often, on a Sunday, you boys would walk down to her nursing home, either alone or with me, and push her back to the house for lunch. It was uphill and it must have been quite scary the way you rattled her up to the front door, but she never complained. She once told me that had a secret ambition to be a racing driver, an idea I simply could not contemplate. I didn't even think she was a good driver! I once took her to Green Lanes shopping centre in Barnstaple and let go of the handles of the wheelchair while I looked in Dorothy Perkins shop window. 'I'm going,' she said in a quiet voice, then with more urgency, 'Ninette I'm going off by myself!' I had to grab her before she disappeared down the mall never to be seen again. She obviously didn't fancy racing around the walkways of a shopping mall in a wheelchair.

It's never easy when you're young, having to watch an old lady who's had a stroke, trying to eat her food and getting in a mess. Do you remember those Sunday lunches in South Molton? Roast dinners eaten around the kitchen or dining room table. The conversations would move from boring to the bizarre with Grandma and your dad.

'How's that dog of yours Eileen?' your dad would ask.

'Amber died donkey's years ago Gerry.'

'I remember when you turned down a visit to the theatre and dinner because you'd lost the dog.'

'Well, that was when I still lived in Ickenham in the 1970s.' She pauses for thought. 'What year is it now Ninette?'

'Two-thousand and two Mum.'

'Well the bloody dog would be over thirty then.'

Grandma was pretty bright, nothing wrong with her brain, but from the waist down together with most of her left side, her body had given up. She could still crack a joke and she could manage to lift a glass to her lips without spilling too much. The family reckoned that when she eventually passed on, Grandma was going down with a gin and tonic in her hand. She had a wonderful sense of humour which she passed on to her children. Uncle Tony, Auntie Jean and I stood around her bed once because she'd had a relapse and the doctors thought she might be in a rapid decline so we all raced to be with her.

'When I die,' she said, 'I want you all around me.'

'Well, we're all here now, so you'd better get on with it,' Uncle Tony replied. We all held our breath while there was a short pause, then she laughed. The three of us gave it all we could until we were crying with laughter. Grandma did recover that time. As you know, she outlived your dad by two years. When I told her that he'd gone she asked, 'How many of us are left now?' she carried on living beyond many of her oldest friends until she was ninety-one. Having a grandma the same age as your dad must have seemed odd.

We always had good Sunday lunches in every house we lived in. At times there were five children plus extended family around the table and there would be at least one vegetarian. I swear you kids drew lots to see whose turn

37

it would be next to take on a special diet. Your phase of vegetarianism lasted some years, from when you were about nine until you began working as a chef. 'I feel I ought to eat meat if I'm going to be a chef. I mean, I should be able to cook and taste everything not just what I like to eat.'

I closed my eyes to what went on in that huge town house with ten bedrooms. 'Let's all go round Tosh's, his mum's great and we can hide away in the top rooms and she won't have a clue what's going on'. I wasn't stupid, just ignored things, turned the other way. I was pretty naive about drugs at the time and didn't recognise the smell of weed. I should have recognised it from my youth as it was everywhere then, but I never smoked it.

I never took much notice of your involvement in graffiti. I was embarrassed that you did it and like most people hated that tagging thing the street guys do on walls, post boxes, telephone boxes and so on. I couldn't believe a son of mine would desecrate buildings and daub rubbish over public buildings. It's really since you left that I have taken the trouble to find out more about the graffiti conventions. Very unlike the conventions of bridge or chess, but I believe there are rules and regulations. I never realised that a 'piece' painted in a public place is temporary. It never stays there for long and tradition has it that another artist will paint over the top of it and that is perfectly okay in the world of street art. I don't think that happens in the case of Banksy and I wish now that some of your work was still up there for everyone to see. There are photographs of course. Hundreds of them, on the Internet and on your friends' computers. I spent a whole morning looking for GORF and FIBER googling the tags and seeing what came up. I know where GORF came from because you told me that it's FROG backwards, and is slang for a French person — for Laure I expect. I don't know what FIBER is though.

There is a lot out there on the Internet. From your late teens you were never without a sketch pad. Constantly drawing designs for new pieces. One of your friends said, 'Tosh was so good at transferring from sketch pad to the wall he never had to do a rough outline before he began. He could just look at the small page and see it enlarged on the wall without drawing any guidelines. Talented. It's an obsession really, an obsession.'

We tried to get you to paint more on canvas but that would never have worked. It was the buzz of the graffiti as much as anything else that you loved. At home in Dorset, I have a painting that you did of a dinosaur kind of character. I love him and it makes me smile to look at him. He's on the wall behind my head where I sit and work, in my study on the landing. There are other photographs on my wall too: a few of GORF graffiti, and a great caricature of you holding a beer, a spray can and a cigarette; all very much part of you, your uniform if you like.

Love you Tosh.
Mum xx

Chapter Six

17th December 2020

Dear Tosh,

The French lockdown has lifted a little. On the 15th December they increased the distance we could travel. We can now drive anywhere in France and for any length of time, except that the French have brought in a nationwide curfew from 8pm until 6am, which I think is quite sensible. But, there are still no cafés, bars or restaurants open. We also have to wear a mask all the time when outside our own house. We have become used to staying at home, only taking a few hours each day to go out, and not going very far. I think it's a bit like being institutionalised, where you do the same thing every day until eventually it's difficult to break the habit. Yesterday morning, the sun was shining and we'd taken the dog out for her usual walk, we'd had breakfast: bacon and egg and fresh bread, which Geoff had collected from the *Boulangerie*. While finishing our cups of tea and pondering about our respective jobs for the day, Geoff pipes up with, 'Right, come on, we're going out. We can leave the dog for a few hours and I have a hankering to see Mèze and Marseillan. I have no special plans for today'. I was a little reluctant to go. An agoraphobic hand was forcing me to stay put, but the good weather was tempting, and both towns are only around a thirty-minute drive away. I took a deep breath, quickly freshened up and changed my dog walking clothes for something a little more, *going outy*. I grabbed my backpack complete with money, sanitiser, and mask — you can't leave the house now without the last two items — slung it in the car, and we were off. The dog pulled a long face as we shut the door on her but I know she sneaked onto the sofa for a cosy couple of hours as soon as we left. We always leave her a biscuit to eat while we're gone, to ease our guilt about abandoning her for a few hours, but she never touches it until we return. Funny dog. I so wish you could have met her.

We went first to Mèze, parked up close to the water's edge where there were rows of fishermen's nets hanging on wooden frames. They stank of the sea, fish and the tar that stops the rope from rotting. I think they were for catching mussels, which seem to be the main source of local fishing. Oysters are local too, but I don't like those. Once again, my mind dashed into Tosh memory mode. It never fails. Anything to do with food or graffiti and my mind gravitates to you. I imagine you talking me through cooking *moules marinières* served with a green salad and some chips on the side. Do you remember when you had to work for Heston Blumenthal for a week at his pub, The Hind's Head in Bray? You were the vegetable chef and learned how to double or was it triple fry chips? I don't think you were too impressed with Heston although you thought his cooking was good. I'm sure that's what put you off working in service as opposed to catering. You liked preparing food but the hassle of working in a kitchen as a chef under pressure to get the meal onto the table in a restaurant, was too much for you. You disliked the hierarchy in the restaurant business. I worried about you all the time when I imagined the boss shouting at you because you hadn't got table number four's main course ready in time. I don't like the idea of anyone shouting at any of my children, for any reason.

We left the nets wafting with their floats gently banging on the wooden frame in the breeze and soaking up the sunshine, and went for a quick walk around the town. It was typical of an out of season holiday place, dead, empty streets, and there weren't even any bits of rubbish drifting around. A sense of sadness hung about like a mist the heat couldn't lift. It probably seemed worse this year as no restaurants, bars or cafés are allowed to open. When we'd walked around most of the streets in Mèze we found ourselves back at the car. I was desperate for the loo and there was nowhere in sight and I couldn't even see a place to hide behind down by the water so we drove quickly on to Marseillan. Luckily, we parked in a car park beside a public toilet. I made Geoff stand right outside the door, because here they are strange things that lock without having to touch anything. I once panicked because I thought I couldn't get out. It was a relief for me to be able to go to the loo, and this time I was ready for the automatic flush, which practically floods the whole cubicle. I don't know why I'm telling you this. I suppose I thought it would amuse you.

Ablutions over, we looked around for somewhere to begin our exploration of the little town. The shops were all closed, not just because of the virus restrictions but because it was lunchtime and the Europeans always take long lunch breaks. We headed towards the sea, walking down the tree lined streets and taking in the French architecture: tall buildings, beautiful wooden front doors;

some carved and with ornamental door knockers, small wrought iron balconies outside tall windows overlooking the squares and street. I'm loving France more every day and wish so much that you were living here somewhere.

When we arrived at the harbour area I allowed myself the luxury of indulging in nostalgia. Memories of our holidays in Devon. There was something about Marseillan that reminded me of Dartmouth. The quay, the shops, the restaurants beside the water and most of all the clanking of the sheets as the boats rocked on their moorings, which was also a familiar sound in Dartmouth and in Dittisham, where our holiday house was. Of course, none of the restaurants were open, but a few were serving takeaway, which added a little bit of life to them; they had blackboards outside advertising the menus, and gingham tablecloths on some of the tables. Holiday towns in Devon always have blackboards with ice-cream varieties or Dish of the Day written on them.

Geoff walked off to find the Noilly Prat centre. Marseillan is the home of the French Vermouth. I know you might find it odd for Geoff to be interested in anything to do with alcohol as he doesn't drink, but it's the history of the buildings that he always wants to discover, and in this case, also the history of the company. Noilly Prat is a fortified vermouth, not my cup of tea, it tastes of weird herbs and has a fragrance about it that puts me off drinking it. I walked away from the restaurants and around to the other side of the harbour where I sat on a bench, closed my eyes and lifted my face to the sky. I thought about Bayard's Cove Dartmouth, and the history surrounding the town. I know nothing about the history of Marseillan but as I sat I thought about the past and the thousands of people who must have walked on the cobbled streets, working and living their lives here.

They have all passed through this world, just as we are. Everyone must come and go, some of us sooner than others. I won't be here forever, and I know I must make the most of the time that I have. I allowed myself the time to enjoy the feeling this little town gave me, reminding me of my children, all of them, loving the holidays in Devon, swimming in the cool waters at Blackpool sands — I still wonder why a beach near Dartmouth is called Blackpool — then hobbling back across the pebbles to find towels and warmth in cuddles. Walking the streets of Dartmouth, going into the bookshops, the gift store and the cafés. The smell in the air was reminiscent of harbours all over the world, but the scent filling my nostrils yesterday morning reminded me of crabbing. Sitting on the Dittisham pontoon with buckets of water at the ready, in which to plunge the captured crabs by the dozen. Those poor crabs never learnt their lesson; every season, caught several times over, by many different children on their holidays. You and the twins were tutored by your older siblings in the finer details of which bait is the best. Bacon rind was favoured. The competition between you and the twins was hot. The memory put a smile on my face. Wellingtons dirty with sludge from the river banks were chucked on the kitchen floor by the backdoor of the house. Wet clothing, not from rain but from river water mixed with sea-water, peeled off and thrown into the always overflowing washing bin. The smell I could taste in my mouth from the fishing nets yesterday, was the same smell that clung to the walls of the always damp, utility room. You were lucky children, never really spoilt — though some might disagree.

I love you.
Mum xx

Chapter Seven

January 1st 2021

Dear Tosh,

Well, it's arrived, 2021. Everyone is sick of 2020 and we're all hoping for a better 2021.

Geoff and I did nothing yesterday for New Year's Eve. We spoke to our respective families in England and sent a message to Matthew in Thailand. Everyone is locked down all over the world.

I've never been a fan of New Year's Eve. It's always a bloody let down. I have spent a fortune on food and wine in a few fancy hotels. Most notably (and possibly not a let-down) was 2006/7 when Geoff and I spent New Year in Gstaad, Switzerland, with our friends the Leishmans who live there. They had known your dad for years and stayed close to me after he died. We don't see much of them but I would call them close friends. That New Year was perhaps one of my most memorable. I have no idea how much it cost but when Geoff told me the bill for the fizzy water alone was 150 euros or thereabouts, my jaw literally dropped. I always think of you when life involves food and this was no exception.

I must have told you about it. I can't remember the actual menu but what I do recall is that the food never stopped coming and after midnight, having already consumed enough calories to feed an army, they brought out Swiss soup and so many lobsters that they must have emptied the Atlantic Ocean of the crustaceans. I love lobster, don't you? I can't help thinking, as I'm looking back, what a decadent New Year that was. Too much food and probably a great deal wasted. But, the point is, it was memorable; especially when the locals paraded around the hotel at midnight playing the massive cowbells.

This year most of the world have stayed at home for New Year's Eve. Geoff and I played cards, watched a film on the TV, spoke to Emily, Daryl, Evie and Orla on FaceTime for half an hour. We also chatted to Wills in London on FaceTime. It's a good platform to be able to see and talk to family and friends. I messaged Matthew in Thailand and Joe in Bristol — he doesn't go in for too much online socialising. I chatted to you too, in my own head, and a little bit out loud. I generally have a bit of a chat with you every day; telling you about the walk I'm doing; mentioning the weather, keeping you up to date, keeping the memory of the good times going and bearing the pain of loss by trying to connect to you in some way. I don't believe that you can hear me, I don't believe that you can see me, but I do believe it helps my mental health if I keep speaking to you. For quite a lot of the time I ask where you might be, which is ridiculous because I don't think you're anywhere. I can understand why others turn to religion when they feel like this, but I cannot do that, even if I thought it would help.

We are missing out so much on the food that France

has to offer. We've been here since October and not been able to eat out once. We've found a good company that do outside catering and they prepare really good takeaway food. We've had Thai, Indian, and we had a selection of dishes for Christmas, some of which were still in the fridge for last night. I had a bottle of Crémant and Geoff had a non-alcoholic beer or a NAB as we've begun to call them in the family. It was a quiet evening and today, I'm thinking of you more than ever as we approach 14th January 2021.

I was wondering how much of each week you painted graffiti. Was it every day, a couple of times a week or only once a week? If I had to guess I'd say you did something to do with graffiti every day. A sketch, a sneaky painting behind a wall. I was also wondering how many dangerous places you scouted out. Were you one of those who climbed the bridges on the motorway? I know there are some photographs that Wills took of you painting under the M32. How lucky were you not to have had an accident? Was it only a matter of time before you did? You must have been aware that you put yourself in danger not just from the law but from some dreadful calamity. I could ask your friends and painting companions but it's probably better that I don't, and didn't know. My imagination runs all over the place thinking of you hanging off high places in the middle of the night, running down railway tracks and just getting off before the high-speed train came along. I know this is all in my mind but something tells me I'm not far out in guessing the kind of things you might have been up to and I never even realised.

I'll write again soon. In fact, in total, I'm going to write you twenty-seven letters. One for each year and this is only number seven so another twenty to go. Aren't you lucky?

Love you
Mum xx

Chapter Eight

13th January 2021

Dear Tosh,

Last night, I kept thinking about you and what you might have been doing ten years ago at this time. You would have been at the airport, waiting to board the plane to Porto. I sat on the sofa, trying to focus on a TV programme but all I could see were images of you walking through to the gate, backpack swinging, your earphones plugged in, listening to some music on your phone. There was probably a bit of a bounce in your step even though you were nervous about flying. You had almost cancelled the trip because you didn't want to fly and I also think you were nervous about socialising and not having a drink. You spoke to Geoff and me not long before you went to Porto and we both told you not to go if you weren't sure. We should have been more definite in our advice. You also had trouble getting to the airport by all accounts. Missed buses, confused instructions about meeting up.

I wish now that I had reached out, told you not to go. 'Turn back, go home to Exeter,' I should have shouted.

Like I should have called my dad back and given him those bloody sweets.

Last night I could see my boy, innocent of the events that would occur in less than eighteen hours. The emotions were swilling, churning at my stomach and in my head, and to control them, for a while I allowed myself the indulgence of imagining it hadn't happened – I often do that, but I can only make it last for a few seconds. I woke up at seven this morning, and my first thoughts were, 'this time ten years ago, Tosh was already sleeping, and I didn't know, but I was about to find out'. I began to relive the hours following that first phone call. The call that was going to change everything. The moment I knew you had been in an accident. I recall now how my thoughts raced around. It took a while for me to process the information and for it to sink into my stupid head. At first, I was not registering how bad things were.

Joe rang us in the early hours of Thursday morning. It was so early I hadn't heard my mobile ringing as I had left it in the kitchen; only when I got up at seven and walked through to the bathroom did I see four missed calls and a text message: *Mum, can you ring me now please.* It had been left at five-thirty in the morning. I thought that it might be about you, and I imagined Joe was having a problem with you because you were having an episode. That's what we called it when, for some reason, you drank too much and the 'other' Tosh came out. But then, I thought, you had been so much better, no alcohol for four or five months and you were attending counselling sessions, this time with someone you felt confident with, and who made sense to you. It couldn't be you. It must be Joe, up to some stupid practical joke that had backfired so he was calling me from a police cell because he needed rescuing. Mind you, Joe often sent, *can you ring me now* texts and mostly it would be something trivial he wanted to know: the rules of a card game, how to cook pasta or the answer to a quiz question. But, it transpired that Joe wasn't ringing about any of those things. He was phoning to tell us that something dreadful had happened to you in Porto.

I picture you arriving in Porto, pleased with yourself for making the flight and not having to phone your mum before you boarded. You're laughing and chatting with your mates, looking forward to a few days of fun and 'painting'. You check into the hostel where you're going to stay. This would have been around nine in the evening. After wandering around the narrow, cobbled Porto streets, you end up outside a bar where there's a man altering the designs on coins, making them into attractive trinkets. You notice that one of the coins is a French euro with an angel on it. The perfect gift for Laure. You wait outside to buy it while the others go into the bar. When you eventually finish your bargaining, you go inside. The other lads have already bought a round of drinks including a bottle of beer for you.

'I've not had a drink for several months,' you say, 'but I guess one won't hurt.'

After a couple of rounds you all think it would be a good idea to search out some sites for graffiti for the following day. After all, that's the reason you are in Porto; to paint. You find a wall to sit on, a low wall by the side of a building, laugh and joke and take a small amount of coke. I wish you hadn't although everyone told me it didn't contribute to the accident. You're not drunk and you're not drugged, just happy. It's important to think that you were happy, but for me it is hard to believe that the few drinks and a little coke didn't make a difference. Exactly how much of each, I'll never know, and I don't want to know.

Why did you decide to climb up on the roof to see what was on the other side? Did you think you might find the railway line? Why did you do it in the dark? Why did you, and not one of the others decide to explore and look for a place to paint the next day? I think of this moment over and over again. The familiar, *if only this*, *if only that*, those phrases that replay continuously in the minds of the bereaved.

You scramble across the roof, aiming for the apex but before you get there you slip. You crash through a skylight that you don't see, because the roof is covered in muck and leaves. Your legs and body go first. I imagine you try to grab the edges, but you can't. You're looking up. Maybe you shout, 'Fuck, fuck!' Did a hundred memories rush through your head? Did you think of me, of Laure, of the family? Or, did you just think, *shit, I'm going to fall*. You didn't think, *shit, I'm going to die*. I'm sure of that. There wasn't time. You drop to the concrete floor twenty feet below. I see you lying there in the recovery position. Sleeping on your front, head to one side. You snore. The friends who were with you at the time, told me that when they found you, you were snoring. Not yet dead but gone.

A few years after your accident, I was watching a TV detective drama. A man fell to the ground from a window. He landed on his back with one leg bent right underneath him. It occurred to me rather rationally, as I watched, that you had probably ended up like that. Not on your front at all, not cosy, but splayed, like someone shot with a bullet big enough to throw them backwards. I cried at the sight of that man on the television that night, and had to switch it off so that I needn't look at the image.

There are so many little things that stir my memories and emotions every day. Sometimes, it might be something that someone says. They don't want to upset me, they just don't realise the significance of their words, but certain random expressions upset me now when they would never have bothered me before. One of them is when a person says something like, 'the meal was delicious, the dessert was to die for'. A perfectly harmless saying, and one which I may well have used in the past, but one which grates on me now. I always think, how can anything be good enough *to die for*? When I hear people moaning about their children, whether young or old, I think, *don't be like that. You never know when something might happen, when you could lose them forever.* But human nature is what it is. Ten years on, I moan about your brothers and sister sometimes and know that I shouldn't. I also worry more about them now. Since you left, it has made me more aware of the possible hazards that lurk around every corner. Before your accident, I was one of the, *it'll never happen to me* brigade. Now, I know how pathetic and unsubstantiated that theory is. It can happen to anyone and does happen to everyone. Whatever ladder in life they are on, whatever creed, colour, gender etc., nobody is immune from the many causes of death and loss. Unfortunately, death is part of life. You cannot have one without the other. When Joe or Wills go travelling now, I worry. When Emily flies off to New York to work, I worry. When Matthew, far away in Thailand goes off on his hiking adventures, I worry. Now, I can also worry about my grandchildren and Geoff's children and grandchildren. But, you know what? I cannot keep them all in boxes and stop them from living their own lives the way they wish. 'Don't waste your energy and emotions on things that you cannot control or do anything about,' Geoff says. He's right. I have to bottle up my worries and let everyone be. The odds against it happening to me again are probably quite high. After all, this is the second time in my life that there has been a sudden tragedy. The first, of course was when my father, your grandfather, died suddenly in that car accident back in 1963. He never lived to see any of my children or to witness me marrying his best friend. Ain't life strange Tosh? Ain't life strange? But I truly know that *it will never happen to me* is a fool's theory.

Tomorrow is your anniversary. We don't have anything planned this year although all the family should have been together. I imagine we'll see each other on Zoom, talk about you and just remember. I'll write again tomorrow and tell you exactly what we did.

Miss you, as ever.
Love
Mum xx
P.S. Zoom is like Skype or FaceTime (which I think you knew about) and has become all the craze since lockdown as we can no longer hold face to face meetings and people are asked to work from home. It's a video link but you can have hundreds of people attending at a time.

Chapter Nine

14th January 2021

Dear Tosh,

'It's windy out there.' That was a phrase of yours when you were just a boy. You would say it if you didn't want to go outside. It was windy today in the South of France. Very windy and I heard your little voice repeating, 'It's windy out there Mummy, stay inside'. But we didn't. It was the tenth anniversary today, and I felt emotional throughout the whole day. There was a blanket of sadness that didn't even blow away when we went out to Agde, a seaside town about half an hour from here. We walked around a deserted, sorry looking town with buildings made from dark grey basalt. I was not impressed. Maybe, in a normal non-covid year and on a less windy day, it might have shown us a better side. We headed on down to Cap d'Agde, the port of the town, and it wasn't much better although the sky was a brilliant blue and the boats in the harbour looked lovely in the sun. All the shops, restaurants and bars of the quayside were shuttered up and it looked like the day after the Apocalypse. Particularly eerie was a big white Ferris wheel, standing still with the cabins swaying in the wind.

The atmosphere was unsettling but fitting for my mood as I thought back over the events of January 14th 2011.

When Joe spoke to us on the 13th he told us that he, Wills and Laure were all travelling to Porto that day, and that the doctor from the hospital would be phoning me some time during the morning. We waited ages for the doctor to call. I don't think, even when she spoke to me that the seriousness of what had happened actually sank in. I had asked how bad you were and the doctor replied, 'Well, he has a broken leg but that's the least of his problems. He has suffered some trauma to his head. In this country we … how can I put it? …we would say he is brain dead.'

I don't know what I replied but I remember her urging us to get to Porto as soon as we could. I was totally stunned. It was like: *Okay, brain dead. Let me think what that means. Will he be in hospital for a long time? I should get to see him. I wonder if he'll be okay. What should I take with me? For how long should I go?*

I searched for flights on the internet and at first I was going to travel on my own. *I'd be alright, no need for both of us to go.* What a ridiculous idea.

'I must come with you. You can't go on your own. Whatever are you thinking about? Don't be bloody ridiculous.' Geoff urged me to book two flights. There was a daily flight from Bologna to Porto. We had missed it for that day as it was a two-and-a-half-hour drive to the airport. The first available flight we could book was the following day around lunchtime. Unbelievably, I booked return flights. Out on the Friday and back the following Wednesday. I couldn't think straight. What the fuck did I imagine that *brain dead* meant? Was I just going to pop over to Porto, kiss it all better and come home again? I didn't break down, I didn't collapse in a heap of sobbing human distress. I just got on and made a few arrangements and called the family. I was on another planet. When everything had been arranged, Geoff and I went down to the nearest beach and walked with the dog. I began to understand but I didn't really begin to feel. I know everyone reacts differently on these occasions, but when I see reactions portrayed in films or TV series, I'm always amazed that the recipient of tragic news immediately collapses, or bursts into paroxysms of grief. I think — and I know I could be wrong — that the first reaction from most people is that of disbelief or denial.

We flew from Italy to Porto to see you in the intensive care unit at the hospital. It was surreal. Like taking part in one of those hilarious videos that you, the twins and Simon used to make. I looked at you in the bed, a neck brace on, wired up to machines and a horrible fat tube dragging down the corner of your mouth. It looked so uncomfortable and yet you seemed peaceful. Just sleeping. I was sure that at any moment you would open your eyes, and Simon would pop up from behind the bed, and shout, 'Got you there, Mrs Hartley!'

After seeing you in that state, we were ushered into the office with the doctor and a social worker. The staff were kind but business-like; they gave me something, a sedative, 'to take away the butterflies', but they wanted me to sign the papers to agree to donate your organs. It was such a terrible few hours. I'll never forget it and I'm right back in the thick of it now as I write to you about it all.

Your beautiful Laure tells me she thinks you'd definitely want to do that, as you had both recently watched a TV programme on the subject. I try to reach the rest of the family by phone. Matthew is flying in from Singapore and I just manage to speak to him and he says, 'Whatever you think Mum'. Emily is coming from Australia, but Joe speaks to her while she is on stopover in Singapore. She tells him that she was sure you would want to donate your organs.

Ultimately it is up to me as I am *next of kin*. It should be Laure. I hold her hand. I ask Geoff what he thinks. I need him to look at the brain scan. I can't look at it, but I need to know that you are completely dead. I don't believe them. He takes the print-out from the doctor who explains it to him, as I turn my head away.

'He's gone Ninette. There's nothing there. The doctor's told me that the scan is colour coded. Red for activity and blue for less active or not active. It's all blue Ninette. It's all blue.'

I can't stand the idea of them cutting you up. Surgery after death, or possibly before they actually turn off the life support machine.

'Will you sedate him? Will you give him an anaesthetic?'

'Mrs Hartley, your son is more deeply sedated than we could ever make him with drugs.' I hope they are right. They are the experts after all so I have to believe them.

The social worker is a complete wanker. Sorry, there's no other word for it. He's pushing for us to sign, and in an attempt to hurry us up he says, 'You must do this quickly. Every day your son is here in intensive care is costing thousands of euros'. He raises his eyebrows and I can't see the connection between the cost of the hospital and donating your organs. At the same time, I'm horrified to think that he might be trying to blackmail us. What does he mean? Is he trying to scare me?

The doctor interrupts before the wanker can say anything else. 'Mrs Hartley, it is imperative that we work quickly. Your son has already been here more than twelve hours and his body is deteriorating.'

I can't believe I'm in this situation. I'm trying to make a major decision about you, when I've been given drugs, and people in the room only care about having your body to slice into sections and use as spare parts. I can't think straight. I really have no choice. I know you would want to be helping someone else. That was your nature. I look around the room at the expectant faces of the staff and the wrung-out faces of my family.

I sign the paper.

It's Friday night and I am exhausted after the longest day of my life. The hospital says we should go home and come back in the morning before ten. That night they would have to make a lot of final tests.

'The law sets out certain tests we must do before we can declare him dead. We will do that this evening,' says the doctor. What the tests are, I can only imagine. Poking and prodding you, sticking sharp pins in the soles of your feet. Or worse.

Saturday morning comes and I sit beside the bed again. Look at you. Kiss you and tell you I love you. You look better today I think. They've taken the neck brace off and you're dressed in a clean hospital gown, ready for an operation. Only there is no surgery that will make you better. I whisper close to you. 'At least I don't have to worry about you anymore.' I stroke your strong arms and hold your hand. At that moment, I hate graffiti and what it had meant to you. You lived for 'painting' and you bloody died for it too.

A nurse comes up to us. Geoff is standing close to me but giving me plenty of space. He's there if I need him. Laure, Joe and Wills have gone.

'Mrs Hartley. It's time.'

They want me to hurry up. They want to take you away. To wheel you off through the doors of the intensive care unit. I have no choice. I have to let you go.

'Goodbye,' I say and give your hand a squeeze. But the tears don't come. They have given me more drugs — Valium I think — I'm floating a little.

I miss you Tosh.
Love
Mum xx

Chapter Ten

15th January 2021

Dear Tosh,

I said I would tell you what the family did on your anniversary. We didn't have a family Zoom meeting online. We sent messages to each other on the family WhatsApp group. I spoke to Wills and Emily on FaceTime. The best thing of all was that Evie and Orla made a chocolate cake for you to celebrate, or should I say for them to celebrate. It wasn't hugely successful in terms of baking, and looked a bit like a large cow pat.

'He would find it funny Mum,' Emily said, 'and the girls want to put candles on it.'

I suggested ten candles would be a good idea then Emily said, 'Guess what the girls have decided to call it?'

'I've got no idea. Cow-pat cake?'

'No, it's a deathday cake. Get it? Like, birthday cake is for the day you are born, and a deathday cake is for the day you die.'

We laughed at the absurdity of it. I think it's rather sweet and extremely healthy that Evie and Orla can talk openly about death. I'm not sure a 'deathday' cake would catch on with the general public though.

Evie is fascinated by the Mexican, *Día de los Muertos*, Day of the Dead. It's a festival to remember your lost loved ones. A joyful occasion when they might cook the favourite meal of the departed one and make offerings of sweets and food to them; to feed their souls. Dancing, dressing up and singing with brightly coloured costumes. Evie loves painting her face white like a skull, and putting on black eye make-up and very red lipstick. The Mexicans also believe, and so do I, that if you continue to talk about the person you have lost, you keep their memory alive. I read somewhere that you die twice in this world, the first time when you leave and the second time when people stop talking about you. People do still talk about the ancient Greek writers, or Shakespeare, or Julius Caesar, so it's easy to see where this idea has come from.

Evie and Orla wear odd socks to school on your birthday and insist on having a birthday cake for you too. For the last few years it's been a Colin the Caterpillar cake from M&S along with several walnut whips; a favourite of yours I believe? I know they tell their school teachers all about you. You may not be as famous as Julius Caesar, but we try. Uncle Tosh is well known in Bristol that's for sure and not just for graffiti.

I put photographs of you on social media today, and many friends and members of the family commented about what a great chap you were, and how missed you are. They put little red heart symbols by your photograph to signify love. We all did our own thing and thought of you in our own way. I would give anything to hug you today, but I can only be with you by looking at your photograph; closing my eyes and imagining your presence. It's hard to smell you now though. What I mean is, I can't conjure up a smell from nowhere, but occasionally a waft of after shave will cross my path and I think, 'Tosh'. It's quite likely that a whiff of cannabis or patchouli would catch my attention these days — I've learnt to identify it in my old age. The smell of spray paint definitely makes me think of you.

Back in Portugal in 2011, we didn't know what to do with ourselves over that first weekend. Matt and Emily arrived from Singapore and Sydney on Saturday, but too late to see you in the intensive-care-unit. Laure's parents had joined us; they had arrived from France at some point. I had forgotten that Laure's mother was Portuguese and her cousin and his wife lived in Porto. Lucky for us that they did. Although lucky doesn't seem to be quite the right word. They were such a help to us; translating, and taking us around to the various places we needed to visit. It would have been much more difficult without them. They were such wonderful people and gave us so much support in those very early days. Did you ever meet them at all? I must ask Laure.

None of us could speak a word of Portuguese. I thought it was meant to be like Spanish but no, nothing like it. I'll tell you something now that will make you laugh. When Geoff and I got on the plane from Bologna to Porto they made an announcement from the flight deck and I said to Geoff, 'Why are they speaking Polish?' He replied, 'I don't know, maybe lots of Poles travel from Bologna to Porto.' This was of course a ridiculous thing to say, but at the time I just agreed. Portuguese is the most extraordinary language; it looks like Spanish when it's written but sounds more Slavic when spoken. I won't be trying to learn it, I have enough to do keeping up with French at the moment.

Laure's relations had booked us all into the Ibis hotel, which was just behind the hospital. I would describe the

63

hotel as a step up from a hostel; nothing wrong with it just very basic. We stayed there for five nights. Our room felt like a cell and it had a musty smell to it. But the Internet worked and frankly, I probably wouldn't have even noticed had we been staying at the Porto Ritz, if there is one. It became our base, our home, for the time we were there. We completely took over the bar and foyer, and most days there were at least ten of us. We hung around the hotel, wandering aimlessly down the corridors. It was in the most peculiar location in the middle of a small shopping mall. There was a supermarket and a huge food hall but not many other interesting shops. On one occasion, Emily and I explored various routes around the centre looking for something we could talk about. It only took about ten minutes before we were back where we started, so off we went again, exploring in the opposite direction. There was a book fair on one morning and a variety of books were set out on tables in the middle of the walkway. We all like a good book so we had a rummage through. They were all very odd and mostly in Portuguese. We laughed at the book titles. There was one in particular: *How To Teach Your Dog To Dance*. It was the funniest handbook we had ever seen and we mused as to how you would have loved it, and laughed too. It was full of illustrations of dogs dancing, and instructions on how to get them to perform. I wish we'd bought it. We could have looked at it every year at this time, if for no other reason than to say, 'Remember when we found this and laughed?' To remind ourselves that even during this darkest time we could find humour somewhere.

Saturday and Sunday must have gone by but I can't remember much about them. I did call Uncle Tony, and he asked — as everyone did — if there was anything he could do. At the time I couldn't think of anything, but later, when we were given an estimate for the funeral, I had to call him and ask him to lend us some money. He agreed and sent it without hesitation. I felt so bad that we hadn't got any spare cash to pay for everything ourselves. I felt inadequate: as though I was letting you down. I am so sorry. Money is never important, until you don't have it. At the time we were property rich and cash poor.

We spent so much time in the Ibis we began to talk about *Ibisitis*. Sitting in the bar, staring at each other with nothing to say. The two families, French and English, all on our individual laptops, bursting into spontaneous tears, because the tears came often now and at unexpected times. There was still denial in my heart, but if I looked at a text message from you or if someone called me to say, 'We're so sorry to hear the news' or 'what a wonderful boy he was' or 'it's so sad and he was only twenty-seven', when I put the phone down, I would cry until I was ugly.

Wills took photographs all the time; I'm glad he did because we can look back at them all these years later. Some he took of me are fairly unflattering; grief isn't pretty. The photographs help to jog my memory; I've forgotten so much. We took the metro to somewhere but I can't recall where. I think we went for Sunday lunch, and Wills took photos of us all standing about waiting to board the train: photos on the escalator, sitting on the train, sitting at a table, eating lunch. We hardly spoke a word to each other, all in our own little bubbles of thoughts about you, what had happened and with grief beginning to seep insidiously into our lives. I didn't care about how I looked, where I was going, what was happening. I spent hours in my head going over the events, trying to come to terms with it all. I also spent a great deal of time while I was in Porto floating in a cloud of numbness. I often wonder if I could cope with returning to the city; trying to retrace the movements we took that weekend. I might be able to find the restaurant down by the river, where we had lunch. I could go back to the hospital, and maybe even visit the cemetery. I'm not sure what I would hope to achieve, but one thing about it is, I might feel an extra closeness to you because it was the last place you were alive. There's no chance of visiting Porto at the moment. They have high cases of the virus and their borders are closed.

Last year I went to Paris with Emily for a trade fair, to do with Interior Design, which as you know is her business. We went to London St Pancras to travel on the Eurostar. I felt a massive lump in my chest as we walked around the station and found the platform. I could honestly see you there, backpack and hoody, earphones in etc., — the same vision I could see of you at the airport that time. It was an overwhelming emotion that made me want to touch the handrails on the steps, trace my hand around the back of a restaurant seat, cast my eyes over the departure board, thinking that there was a slim possibility that your hand prints might well be there, however faded they might be. I knew without doubt, that you had visited this station many times, travelling to France with Laure, or on your way to join her. It broke my heart.

Talking of that image of you in your backpack, I cannot tell you how many times after the accident I literally thought I saw you. In the distance, disappearing around a corner, running for a bus. I knew it could never be you but just some young man about your age who wore the same 'uniform', but for a nanosecond I was taken in. Stupid really, but I've read that it is common for people to think they see their loved ones after they've died: walking down the street, on a corner, in a shop. It must be auto-suggestion; you're so desperate to make some kind of contact, to reach out for the possibility that it never happened and the person is still alive.

Once, Emily and I went to a restaurant where you could see through to the kitchen from the eating area. There was a young chef grilling a piece of steak. He was wearing an apron and a white hat. Emily and I looked at each other. 'I know what you're thinking Mum,' she said. We shared a moment of loss together. So many things in our ordinary, everyday lives remind us of you. You'll never be forgotten.

All my love
Mum xx

Chapter Eleven

16th January 2021

Dear Tosh,

Back in Porto in 2011, Monday came. The day of having to 'do' things. We were to meet with the funeral company in the afternoon. In the morning, we were hanging around. I kept thinking of you, imagining you dead and in the morgue. Would you be in a drawer? I'd had no experience of morgues so could only summon up a picture from hospital TV dramas or detective films I'd seen. If I thought too long about your emotions, I worried that I hadn't done enough to care for you, nurture you. Could I have helped you more? Could I have talked more to you about your problems? I just didn't know. My head was in turmoil. I needed to focus on something practical. Geoff and Matt came up with the idea of collecting your things. We had asked on Saturday but had been told we couldn't claim anything until Monday. Geoff, Matt, Emily and I traipsed over to the hospital like a little posse.

The secretary was reluctant to help. We communicated in broken English, a bit of French and some Italian. Then after some confusion over names she said, 'Oh, the young man from England. You are the mother of him who died. We are so sorry'. At which point her whole demeanour changed, and she became helpful and kind. It occurred to me at that point, that the whole hospital would know about you. A young, healthy, handsome man had died in their hospital. Certain staff would have been excited about the prospect of sharing out the spoils. It gave me a bitter taste. I wanted to cry and be sick at the same time. I thought about that wanker of a social worker in the office, and I hated him. Your body parts would have been worth thousands of euros to them. I had to stop thinking like that. You would not have wanted me to be bitter. Besides the young secretary was now being sympathetic towards us, and handling things with care. I kept trying to tell myself, *Tosh wouldn't want us all to be miserable and bitter*. It didn't help much.

We had to go to two different rooms. 'Only the next of kin will be allowed in. That is you.' she said, pointing at me. Both rooms were in the basement of the hospital. It was ghastly down there. A subterranean warren of pipes and vents, echoing with loud clangs and crashes. It had the smell of sanitiser and bleach, a bit like the indoor swimming baths. Sometimes, if a door swung open a rush of warm air would enter the corridor and our nostrils filled with the reek of hot, wet, dirty washing. I had entered another film set, this time a psychological thriller. *One Flew Over the Cuckoo's Nest* came to mind. The corridors were long and busy with people pushing trolleys full of dirty laundry. Steel doors on either side looked ominous. Had I been watching this on a film screen, I would have been hiding behind a cushion. I think the morgue was down there somewhere too. I could not stomach the idea of my beautiful boy being in such a hostile environment and in a situation where I could offer you no comfort. We carried on walking through this endless maze. When we met other staff who might have hindered our progress, our young lady showed them a piece of paper with your name on it and explained why we were there. Each stranger we met became exceedingly helpful as soon as they knew who we were. A look of sympathy would come over their faces and they were courteous, but we still had to do everything by the book. Signing a thousand signatures, it all seemed a bit sordid and clinical and took forever.

The first room I was taken into was not large. It contained a desk and boxed shelving all around the walls. The attendant took the piece of paper, checked my identity and then handed me the black plastic bag containing your clothing. I had to sign for it. A bloody great lump came into my throat. I thought I might be sick. I daren't look inside. I thanked the man/woman, (I can't even remember what gender they were) and rushed out through that heavy door and handed the bag over to Matt, Emily and Geoff. A few doors down the secretary guided me into a similar room. In here, personal items were locked away. This was where the contents of your pockets had been taken. It was the same procedure as the last office but this time they handed over a clear plastic bag. It contained paper money and change and not much else. I remembered that Joe and Wills already had your wallet. By the way, I spoke to Wills the other day and he told me something about that wallet.

'Did you know that Tosh had tried to see me before he went to Porto? He rang me but I just missed his call. I tried calling him back, but he sent me a message saying he was at the airport; the text message said: I have a photograph in my wallet of Laure and of Joe but I don't have one of you. I wanted you to know that before I left and that I love you.' Wills then told me that after the accident when he and Joe were given your wallet they looked in it and found the photos of Joe and Laure. 'Imagine how I would have felt if I'd never spoken to him. I would have been really upset to have been left out.' I found this little anecdote so touching Tosh.

Where was I? Yes, the plastic bag. We immediately searched inside for the souvenir coin but couldn't see it anywhere. I was devastated. It must have been lost. Poor Laure. We had all wanted to find it for her. We made our way back to the hotel. Matt took the black bag to Joe and Wills, and together they went through it.

Afterwards they told me it was evident that your jeans had been cut off, just like they do in the movies. I could hardly bear to think about it. I couldn't cope with the idea that your brothers were all searching through your clothes. They were probably pulling them inside out, probing, rifling. I wanted to be there, I wanted to hold your jumper close, inhale your smell. But I would have been a wreck. I didn't go near them, or your clothes. I waited and tried to remain strong for everybody. At last they came back.

'We've found it Mum! It was pushed inside the tiny, square pocket at the front of his jeans,' said Wills.

'He must have put it there for safe keeping.' Joe could hardly hold back the tears.

We passed the coin around celebrating this magnificent find. We smiled, kissed it, held it up. Then we all looked at each other. What were we going to do with it?

Matt then spoke, he'd had an idea. 'I'll go into town and see if I can find a jewellery shop and buy a chain for it. Then Laure can keep it and wear it. That's what Tosh would have wanted. He would probably have done something similar.'

We all agreed that this would be the best thing to do so Matt bought a chain along with a pretty gift box. It was decided that Wills should give it to Laure and when the right moment came, he took her away from the rest of us, told her that we'd found the coin, and gave it to her without ceremony. She was happy to have it, but devastated.

Geoff put his arm around me. It was time to get back to the Ibis where the funeral directors were waiting for us to choose the coffin. You're going to love that letter when you read it!

Love
Mum xx

Chapter Twelve

17th January 2021

Dear Tosh,

They changed the evening curfew in France yesterday from 8pm to 6pm. Fortunately, it doesn't bother us. We can still do what we want to do during the day and travel wherever we want as long as we're tucked up in our houses by six in the evening. I did venture out today to Lidl. I drove to a store about sixteen miles away, a new one which I wanted to try out. This is what lockdown does to you. The excitement of discovering a new supermarket as a trip out. *Quelle horreur*! What have I come to? Looking around the supermarket shelves as escapist entertainment. Lidl is great for that because they sell a wide range of goods from tools to bread. I spent a little time trying to decide which pastries I should choose: the *pain au raisin* or *pain au chocolat*? Both equally delicious. I also bought bacon, proper looking bacon, which for some reason is hard to find here. Some of the expats truck in loads of it every now and then, but I haven't really had the chance to make contact with them.

Ten years ago, the 17th was the Monday in Porto, and

I was having to make choices of a very different kind. We had left the others, after Wills had given Laure your coin, and Matthew, Emily and I sat with the undertaker in the reception area at the Ibis. She was a lovely young girl called Irina and her English was good. Her manner was professional and she dressed in a smart suit. I think Irina had been trained to appear calm and capable. I can't recall the colour or style of her hair but in my mind, she had a mid-length brown bob and she was not afraid to smile. I suppose she took her cue from the way we were behaving. Irina was gentle and emotional. I think maybe organising your funeral differed from the norm in many ways. We weren't religious for a start. In fact, when I stood by your coffin a few days later, I tried really hard to believe in something. To think that you might be joining your dad somewhere, but it was a scenario I couldn't possibly hold with. As I wrote earlier, I didn't know where you were, but coming to terms with the fact that you might be nowhere, was too difficult for me to contemplate. When I think about it now, ten years on, I know that you are alive in all of us, in all the memories and in almost every family conversation every time we are all together. That's where you are — always in our hearts and minds. Every day, more than once, there is some incident that makes me think of you. Today I was listening to a story on the New Yorker Podcast, while I was walking the dog. The theme of the story is irrelevant, but it had been published in the magazine in 2006. I immediately thought, *Tosh was alive then*. The same happens, if I see a piece of graffiti, or hear a certain song: 'Eternal Flame' by The Bangles for example, was on the radio the other day, you used to sing it when you were very young, only six I think. So many things I hear and see every day in my life make me think of you. By the way, you had a brilliant singing voice. At one stage, West Buckland School wanted you to audition for a scholarship and become a choir boy at Exeter Choir School. I'm sure you would have passed had we allowed you to go. Your dad wouldn't hear of it. He said it would mean that every Christmas, Easter and most Sundays you would have to be at school, singing. He didn't like the idea of that. It would have meant boarding too. I had sent Matthew away to board when he was only eight, and although he doesn't hold it against me now, it made him very unhappy. I realise it was a big mistake. I thought at the time I was doing the best for him, and he did receive a good primary school education, passing the Common Entrance Exam without a problem, but in retrospect, it was a cruel thing to do.

Back to the Ibis, Irina and the arrangements for you. I imagine the majority of her dead clients were old — I don't mean they'd been dead a long time — but she perhaps dealt more with husbands, wives, sons or daughters when planning funerals. She did say to us that you were a special case, and she went out of her way to be helpful. We were a mad, grieving family with volatile emotions, and she engaged with us. I think she might have been somewhere close to you in age, which must have had an effect on the way she behaved around us and helped us prepare for your cremation.

While we sat on identical, hotel utilitarian chairs, took drinks in plastic cups from the machine in the hotel entrance, Irina gave us a brochure full of funeral paraphernalia — I can't think of a better word for it. Leafing through it was a bizarre experience. I have never been a catalogue person except when I was a single parent living with Matthew and Emily, on the council estate in Weston-Super-Mare. My mother used to use one, and she always left it with me so that I could browse through and look for anything from school shoes to baking tins, underwear and bog-standard track suits. Stuff like that. Looking at coffins and their accompanying bits and bobs, reminded me of that time. Buying things on tick. Choosing something, and then making a weekly contribution until it was paid for. Of course, coffin shopping was quite a different experience.

The mind is a phenomenal piece of equipment. Like most people, I am unable to control my emotions if my brain sends messages. I've tried yoga, deep breathing, concentrating on a spot on the horizon or other such tricks. I don't think I'm any different to anyone else in that if something seems ridiculous, funny or dreadful, I lose perspective. Discussing coffins with my two eldest children seemed surreal. What on earth were we doing? We were trying to focus, and this exercise was supposed to help us. We found ourselves stifling laughter, which is not an uncommon emotion for the bereaved to experience. At times of grief and deep sorrow, for some reason people begin to giggle. It's a kind of hysteria thing brought on by anxiety, even though you might not feel anxious. I remember, when the family were all in the funeral car, driving along behind the hearse which carried my father, I recognised the road to the crematorium as the road to the swimming baths and I said, 'This reminds me of going swimming'. At which point everyone started to giggle and those giggles turned into laughter.

'It's Daddy making us laugh,' said my mother, and we all agreed. But actually, it was just a perfectly normal reaction and it eased the tension we were all feeling.

Matthew, Emily and I all made comments on the colour, the shape and the style of the handles of each coffin, as though we were choosing items for a fashion shoot.

'Ooh, those are nice, but a bit garish…what about these silver ones?' someone said. 'We definitely don't want gold.' It might have been Emily who said that, but the whole thing was bloody ridiculous. We concurred that it was going to be burnt, without anyone really seeing it as it would happen in Portugal. We also felt that you probably wouldn't give a toss what it looked like and would have preferred to have graffiti plastered all over it. But, we had to be sensible so we picked the plainest box. It was, literally, just a rectangular wooden box that looked as though Geoff could have made it back at the farmhouse. I don't think it even had handles. Matt showed Irina which one we'd chosen. She did seem a little nonplussed, and then told us that it was actually one of the most expensive because it was a replica of the coffin used for Pope John Paul II. It was around €5,000.

'What price?' I couldn't believe it. 'Sorry, we cannot possibly pay that, it's ridiculous.' I was astounded that such a simple box could be that expensive. Just goes to show how an endorsement from a famous person can push up the price.

We huddled back in the corner with the bloody brochure, and began searching again. This time we went for something ghastly, dark wood, with ornate carving and wooden handles. It was also cheap. It was all we could do. This was a Catholic country where coffins and funerals are taken very seriously. Not that we were treating it lightly but the problem was; they don't do that many cremations. Not on a large scale; it's all burials, so everything was ornate, fancy, glossy and just over the top.

I had received the certificate of death and gave it to Irina. She needed it before she could book a slot for your cremation. That sounds awful, like making an appointment with the hairdresser. The thing is Tosh, that when I read it, I was astonished to see that the time stated for your death was 23.55 on the 14th January. I couldn't get my head around this. I had seen you on Saturday morning the 15th, when you were still in intensive care; when as far as I was concerned you were still alive. The date just didn't seem right. But then I began to think about it. The more I thought about it the more I realised that it was a good thing. You hated odd numbers, and somehow, I hoped that you would be happier to be declared dead on the 14th and not the 15th. Later, when I spoke to Laure about it she told me she had experienced the same train of thought. These are such bizarre, random things, but I wanted you to know. We didn't manage to fix any other dates for you with an even number though. Sorry.

Our next problem was what would we do with your ashes? We had the choice of stuffing them in someone's hand luggage and hoping they would get through security or doing the whole thing officially. I couldn't bear the idea that something might go wrong and they would confiscate you before we got on the plane. We opted for the official route which of course involved a ton of money, paperwork and official stamps. It was decided that Matthew would collect you from Heathrow. We chose an elegant marble urn for the transportation. Later, back in England, when you had been decanted into several tea caddies and other containers, so that we could spread you in all the places you loved, we realised the error of paying €300 for the fancy vessel. In the end Geoff and I gave the marble urn to the undertaker in Petritoli. We hoped it would be used by someone who could not afford to buy one for a loved one. We replaced it with a beautiful wooden urn which looked Asian, from an antique shop in Italy. Part of you stayed quietly in that until we brought you home to Bristol, which we eventually did.

A good note to finish on. Bringing you home.

Love
Mum xx

Chapter Thirteen

18th January 2021

Dear Tosh,

Today is the anniversary of my mother's death. Grandma was widowed at the age of fifty. She was the same age as my father, both born in 1913 which was also the same year your dad was born. I bet that fact seems strange to you. If they were alive now they'd all be 108 this year!

When your dad was taken into a secure unit at the hospital in Barnstaple, at the end of 2002, I realised I couldn't cope with visiting him and looking after him as well as looking after and visiting Grandma. I arranged to sell the house in South Molton and move back to Buckinghamshire where Geoff and Anthea would be able to help me from day to day. I thought I would be able to find a place in a secure home for Dad and locate a home for Grandma at the same time. My sister would also be able to help with our mother as Bucks was closer to Thames Ditton than Devon was.

It was sad and a shame that your father died before I could move him. But I had already sold the house in South Molton so I kept my plan to return with you and the twins to Bucks, and I still moved Grandma. I found a nice home on the outskirts of Aylesbury. You of course know all this, but I don't remember ever discussing the details with you at the time. I didn't think you wanted to be involved with all these decisions so I just got on with it all. It was a mission to move her as we had to have a qualified nurse travel with us. I knew most of the nurses at the nursing home in South Molton and one in particular, Karina, was a good friend of yours. You and she were at school together. Karina is one of the friends who always posted on your Facebook page for your anniversary or birthday, or sometimes just randomly. She would post a photo of odd socks or share a photo of graffiti with you. Since you left us, she has also gone. She developed breast cancer, and although she tried to beat it she died at the end of 2019. She showed such courage and strength, always smiling and optimistic to the end. She left behind her husband and two young boys. Karina was terrific with Grandma. It was a long drive from Devon to Buckinghamshire and I was grateful to have her with us in the special transport we had to take. She stayed the night with us and left the next day to return to Devon. Although she and I communicated over the next few years, I do believe that was the last time I actually saw her. It would be nice to think you two were together somewhere having a joke.

Grandma had two years in the home in Aylesbury. She started out in a lovely big room with a view of the lake. But we couldn't afford to keep her in that the whole time. The money she received from selling the house in Weston Super Mare was around £57,000 and it was rapidly diminishing as she had to make a contribution to the care fees. At the time the government allowed a person to keep £16,000 in their personal bank account, any more money than that, had to be used to top up. When the money ran out the council took over, but of course they would only pay the minimum amount. I couldn't bear the thought of Grandma having anything less than the best, but it was impossible for me to continue to top up the fees, as there was so little left. I let the amount go down to almost nothing at which point we had to allow the home to move her into a shared room. I hated it. I felt so guilty. She ended up in a tiny room with only a curtain dividing the room to separate her from the other occupant. It was shit basically; absolutely shit, but I could do nothing about it. The money was gone, and none of the family could afford to keep her in a better place. I asked myself, even at the time, was I wanting to do it for me or for her? I can't answer that. I'd like to think it was for her. Because, even though she didn't have any real control over her limbs anymore, I was sure she was *compos mentis* and I wanted to give her the best surroundings that I could. It was a battle with the authorities because they also held back extra funding, which they could have given her because — believe it or not — they didn't consider she needed *nursing care* only *residential care*. She only needed help with personal care not special medical care. To me this was madness; towards the end she couldn't walk, take care of her personal hygiene, feed herself properly, do anything in fact, but there was no arguing with them.

During her stay in Aylesbury, we did try and take her out as much as possible but it wasn't easy. Do you remember the day we took her to Geoff and Anthea's and we sat in the garden and had tea? We had to pay a nurse to come with us and we had to hire special transport to take the wheelchair, the same as when we moved her from Devon, but this time it didn't cost so much money.

I'm glad we did that for her. It was the last outing she had and the last time she saw you and the family. She didn't say much but smiled, drank the Prosecco and laughed at our jokes. She loved seeing the animals at their place; they had horses, goats and dogs. It must have been in the summer of 2004, the same year that you were twenty-one. We won't go into that again now!

At the end of that year, Grandma had another stroke. I was away in Switzerland at the time. She was taken into hospital in Wycombe and when I got back I went immediately to see her. I had asked Geoff to collect me from the airport. That Christmas, he had come to a party with some other people from the office where we both worked. I was house sitting in a big place belonging to friends, so was able to accommodate several guests. Geoff returned the following evening and we watched a DVD together but that had been the extent of our relationship. Getting him to pick me up seemed a good excuse to see him again, but instead of him driving me home I had to ask him to take me straight to the hospital, which he did. I was a bit disappointed because it brought rather a hasty end to the day. But, he offered to collect me later and — not only that — he also invited me out to dinner at a rather nice restaurant about a forty-minute drive away. It was our first proper date. It was lovely because a few weeks later, when I sat beside my mother in the nursing home and she was fading, I could say, 'I've met someone Mother. I think you would really like him and I think he will take good care of me.' I wanted her to know that I would be okay.

I was with her when she died. Despite the fact that she had asked a couple of years before for all her children to be there when the time came, as it turned out it wasn't practically possible. I sat all day by her side waiting. I had made some tapes of jazz piano music, songs from the musicals and some classical themes. She couldn't speak to me, she had lost that power. She just lay there as the flesh under her finger nails and toenails began to turn blue. There was no joking at her bedside this time. She fought death until the last moment. A nurse came and held me as I held Grandma's hand. Just before she died she lurched towards me with wide pleading eyes. I've never forgotten those staring eyes. I don't think she wanted to go and it made me feel guilty. But it was time, and I couldn't help her. I had asked the doctor the day before if they could give her morphine to gently ease her out of this world but they declined. 'She's not in pain, she will just fade away,' he said. 'We can only administer drugs like that for pain. Just keep her lips moist and give her sips of water.'

In February 2005 you wrote in Grandma's funeral book, *See you soon Grandma*.

Love Mum xx

SKYLIGHT IN THE CLOUDS

Today while out walking
I looked up and — as though
a hand had torn away a rectangle
of cloud — I saw a blue
patch exposing the rough shape
of a broken skylight   not unlike
the one that you fell through

I closed my eyes
and saw your fingers
clinging

When I looked a second time
              a fork of sun
                    flashed down
                          and struck me square.

                          It was over
                                within
                                seconds

Chapter Fourteen

19th January 2021

Dear Tosh,

I told you that when I booked flights from Bologna to Porto I booked returns, but it was soon obvious we couldn't leave on the following Wednesday and it turned out that this would be the day of your cremation, 19th January 2011 (note the odd number). Geoff Hartley flew over from England; he was the only one of the extended family that I wanted there. As your eldest half-brother and only surviving child from your dad's first marriage, it seemed appropriate. At the time, although other close relations made a request to come over, I knew I couldn't cope with more people. I was holding it together very well; you would have been proud of me.

Our return flight was booked for Wednesday morning. My Geoff and I had a long discussion between ourselves and with others and decided that he should return to Italy and I would go back to England. Things needed to be done at the farm and the dog had only been left temporarily with friends. The cremation was arranged for 11am at the Cemitério de Prado Repouso, Porto. By that time in the morning, Geoff Hartley would be with us and I had plenty of support from the rest of the family. I know my Geoff felt bad about leaving me, but we had to be practical about some things. There was no more he could do in Portugal and he would join me later in the UK in time for your memorial service. We chose to hold that at Arnos Vale and The Paintworks in Bristol. We spent the next few days planning and set the date for the 27th January (note another odd number). It was tough parting, but he took a taxi to the airport, and I got on with the day and the next couple of weeks as best I could. It was easy in 2011 to keep in touch by text message, phone calls and Skype and today, it's even easier. We think nothing of speaking to someone and seeing them at the same time. I remember when I was young the idea of video calling was straight out of a science fiction story. 'You mean you'd be able to see someone as you spoke to them on the phone? That's impossible. It will never happen'. I know I actually said that. But, of course it has happened. My father would be incredulous if he could come back and see us now. So much has changed since 1963.

The grounds of the crematorium were peaceful and beautiful, even though it was winter there was plenty of green foliage. I would like to go back one day and see what it is like during the summer. We didn't arrange any kind of service. Yet again the whole thing was surreal. I held on to Geoff Hartley as they brought the coffin to us, I think it was on a trolley. I remember that I couldn't bear to look at you in that box but that I needed to know it was definitely you in there. That you were dead and that was it. I'm guessing you were in a shroud because we didn't buy any clothes for you. It was one of my lowest points of the time in Porto. It was absolute; letting you go to nowhere. I couldn't even bring myself to look at you, say goodbye and kiss you. I was lost. Lost for words, lost emotionally. I don't remember the tears flowing at all but I'm sure they did. Geoff made his way towards the coffin and the lid was lifted. He came back to me, held my hand and told me that, yes, it was you in the coffin. My inability to look at you at that time has left a dark taste in my mouth. I have no idea what I was afraid of. My only consolation is that I know you would not have been upset with me. You would have understood and in your usual compassionate way would have said, 'Don't worry Mum. It makes no difference. I don't have a problem with it and neither should you.' Easier said than done. As I write this now, I ask myself would I feel better about the whole bloody episode of the cremation had I been strong enough to kiss you, to touch your face, which was beautiful? Am I embarrassing you? You were good looking you know. I have a photograph of you, dressed in a suit, walking out of the church after a wedding, and you could easily play the part of James Bond. You were better looking than any of the actors who did.

It was such a sad day. It was almost impossible for me to grasp what was happening. I was there, but it was as though I was only observing everything as it happened around me, and not actually a part of the event. I watched as you were wheeled into a little open-sided stone-built extension, which clung to the side of the incinerator housing. I say housing, but I think it was made to look like a chapel from the outside but only big enough for one body at a time. I've looked online recently, to see images of the place but it appears to have been considerably updated from the way I remember it.

That word, 'Incinerator' is horrible. It pricks the

inside of my head to write it, and it's playing havoc with my colon. I hated the whole idea of you being burned in a furnace. None of it was right. I tried to pretend that none of it was happening. We all stood around you not knowing what to do or say. Matthew thought we should take a turn in saying something. The coffin was draped in white lilies. Each of us mumbled something as we placed a hand or two on top of the casket. There was no priest, no humanist, nothing. This was it. This was the bloody end of pretending that it hadn't happened. The seriousness of the situation hung like a fat rain cloud and reality began to sink in as the cloud burst and drowned me. I have never felt so low. There was a helplessness that weighed down my arms and a complex sense of non-understanding the world we live in; death and life, so closely linked, so tenuous. I know that sounds trite and it's been written and said many times before but I found myself in a situation that made me question everything. It's very easy to ignore mortality and put thoughts of death away in a drawer until you are faced head on with it. Standing there that day I thought about my own death; when, where and how etc. It is not right that a child dies before their parent and I think this is what was playing on my mind the whole time. For you and me the sequence had gone wrong, and it bothered me. Many mothers lose their children and I too had joined that club. I had no choice in becoming a member. None of us did.

'Mum, would it be bad of me to take some photos?' Wills asked. We all agreed that he should. In fact, it is something that I have always thought about when attending funerals. Although at this one there were only the few of us, often many people attend funerals and afterwards, members of the close family, who stumble through the day, cannot remember who came. Except for the cards and signatures in the book if there is one. We needed something to remember the day as our brains were not fully taking it in so we were happy for Wills to click away surreptitiously. I looked at those photographs when Wills sent them to me recently. They are a mixture of sad, odd and amusing in a weird way. There's one of all of us, taken by Laure's father I think, as he's the only one not in it. We look like a cartoon family, a cross between the Simpsons and the Adams family. Honestly, we do. We're trying to smile — don't know why — Matthew looks as though he's an eleven-year-old boffin; I think it's his glasses and the altered perspective, because he's in the front. I'm standing behind him and I look okay, not as though I'm attending the funeral of my son. I have a silly smile on my face. Geoff Hartley is behind me, I can't see his expression. Emily has her arm around Laure and is smiling at her. Laure's mum who is very short, smiling up at her daughter. Joe is having a bad hair day. Wills has a fixed toothy grin on his face and Daryl, all six-foot-five of him, stands on the left of us all with his arm around the twins' shoulders. It looks as though we're trying hard to make the best of a bad moment. It could be a gathering for any family event. I'm glad Wills shared the photo with me, and I'm even more glad that I can laugh about it now. I know you wouldn't be offended. You would have a real belly laugh if you could see it. It's very hard to look at some of the photographs but I make myself do it. It helps me to recall places and people so that I can write to you about it all.

One of the other photographs Wills sent me was of the skylight that you had crashed through. I never went to the site at the time, I left that to the others. Your friends who were there with you took Geoff, Matt, Joe,

Wills and Daryl. Emily and I stayed away. Geoff was explaining to me recently, that the roof was made of corrugated asbestos and the skylight was a piece of clear plastic. I can see that when I look at the image Wills shot. I understand now how you would have put your foot in the wrong place. From the outside, you can't see the difference between the roof and the skylight, the whole area is covered in yellow and green lichen, blending the two different materials into one. From the inside, at least during the day, which was when Wills took the photograph, you can see daylight through the translucent plastic, and not through the asbestos.

I was shocked to see the photo; it's an ugly building. From the side where you climbed onto the roof, the height of the building is deceptive because it's built on the side of a mound; you probably thought it was a long low warehouse, around ten feet in height, but in reality, it was at least twice that. When you moved towards the apex, the drop below was much greater than you might have imagined. But then again, I don't imagine you thought for one second that you were about to crash through. I can't believe you ended up on the concrete floor in such a horrible place; dirty, damp and dingy. It breaks my heart to look at it, and know that the baby I brought into the world, and who was placed in a clean crib with soft white scented sheets, ended up somewhere which was the complete antithesis of that.

A short while after I had looked at that particular image of the cracked roof, I was out walking the dog through the vineyards here in France. I was on my own, as Geoff had some work to do. It was a dull and cloudy day, and I looked up, because I was aware of a sudden brightness. I saw a blue rectangle of sky appear through the clouds — this is going to sound biblical, but it wasn't, it was just an amazing experience. I tried to take a photograph. I was a bit late to capture a true comparison with the skylight you fell through, but a few lines of poetry came into my head which I later wrote down.

After the cremation was over, we left the gardens and walked down into town to a restaurant where a table had been booked for us to eat lunch and try to find some kind of normality. We sat outside on the pavement; the day was quite warm. We ate Portuguese sausage and drank wine. The photographs of this meal look like a couple of families enjoying a normal relaxed meal. Anyone observing our little group could not have guessed the turmoil going on in each of us. But, my insides calmed down as I sat there, and I floated through the rest of the day like a ship without a navigator. We checked out of the hotel, and headed to the airport. Conversation was forced and stilted as we all tried our utmost to pretend that we were managing our emotions and all was under control. Eventually we boarded the flight back to England, where we would stay with Geoff and Anthea for the next few weeks.

Signing off now, feeling a bit sad thinking about that day but trying to remember the love shared by the families, and that you were the centre of it all. Miss you and love you.

Love from.
Mum xx

Chapter Fifteen

20th January 2021

Dear Tosh,

We went for a walk to the Cirque de Mourèze, an area which is millions of years old and erosion has made the dolomite rock into fantastic sculptures and rock formations. Walking was not easy, some of the passages were narrow and I found myself clambering up and down the rocky pathways, using my stick to help me. It's a stick that Geoff made from the bay tree in the garden at the farm in Italy. He honed it, oiled it and polished it then gave it to me for a birthday present at a time when we were a bit hard up. I loved the fact that he made it for me; it's one of the best birthday presents ever. It's really strong and has a natural kink in it at the top which serves as a small handle I can rest my thumb on as I walk. Even with the stick Geoff had to drag me up a couple of awkward places where my legs just weren't long enough or my feet couldn't find any purchase on the craggy sides. Jpeg loved it, and pulled on her lead excited to see around every twist and turn. I had to let Geoff hold her most of the time otherwise she would have dragged me over.

The area was like a film set and reminiscent of a land for dinosaurs. You loved dinosaurs. Once, on your birthday you were given a wooden dinosaur skeleton kit to make. Off you went with your kit to school and not only did the teacher help you make it, she organised a table to make a dinosaur land, with trees and all your plastic dinosaurs. You see how every day my life is punctured with events to remind me of you at every stage of your life. Mrs Carder was the teacher who made the dinosaur land. She lived in a cottage at the end of our drive and still does. She made school a place where you wanted to go, and she loved you and the twins. I think it was Mrs Carder who drew out your love for wildlife particularly bugs and pond life. You spent hours with her in the garden. She also used to do things like dipping bunches of elderflower into batter and frying them. I'm not sure you liked those too much but you were too kind to tell her. She was the perfect primary school teacher, always doing interesting projects with the children and full of enthusiasm for everything her pupils produced. She used to take photographs and keep scrap books, a couple of which she sent to me after you'd gone. One of them has the photos of the dinosaur land you made. I'm not sure she would be able to take all those photographs today. It probably wouldn't be politically correct. But, as a bereaved mother, I treasure them and thank her for the time and trouble she took to prepare them. You were well liked by the teachers at Filleigh Primary School, and why wouldn't you be? A happy, handsome little lad with an enthusiasm for life that most boys have, but that you outwardly showed. If only we could all bottle that energy and zest for living...I could do with opening a pint of it right now.

I was looking back at Facebook - it's a great place to

jog memories and I saw this post that I wrote on the 31st December 2011.

I lost my beautiful son Tosh in January 2011. I don't want his memory to die so don't be afraid to mention his name, in fact if you know anyone who has lost a child whatever their age, don't be afraid to mention them to their loved ones. It doesn't matter if you "don't know what to say" a kind understanding hug, a memory of them, anything, don't shy away from it. Bereavement is not a disease, you can't catch it but those people who are mourning their lost children need to be able to talk about them and keep their memory alive. This is not a post to be copied and passed on, it's just my own thoughts today. 2011 wasn't all bad, my lovely daughter Emily married Daryl, the sun shone and we all celebrated and had a great day.

The year two thousand and eleven was a busy year in our family. Reminiscent of *Four Weddings and a Funeral* but in our case, it was five weddings, your funeral, and your memorial service came at the end of January. Emily had planned to marry in 2011. Remember Daryl proposed to her on Brooklyn Bridge when he took her to New York after our Bristol trip? She said she wanted to get married at our farm in Petritoli.

Emily and Daryl organised everything from Australia, which wasn't easy. Geoff and I were on the frontline and Geoff worked really hard to get the farmhouse into a state fit enough for a country wedding.

He finished the portico with red floor tiles and then the wooden beams which made up the structure surrounding three sides of the house became partially roofed with sail cloth and there were a few traditional coppi tiles over the section above the front door. The beams also supported a terrace accessed from the only inhabitable part of the house, our studio apartment on the first floor. That terrace was an absolute sun trap, almost impossible to sit on during the height of the summer.

One of the other weddings to which Geoff and I were invited, was a real Italian experience. The daughter of a man who took English lessons with me, married an American. Italian weddings are all about the food, English weddings are all about the drink. I'm generalising I know but on the surface that's what it seemed to me. The Italian wedding was held on the coast in the Hotel Fortino in Portonovo. A rather grand affair. Geoff and I were the only non-Italians invited and we felt honoured to be there. We'd brought a present with us, not realising that the Italian tradition is to give money. The bride and groom sat at their own table in front of everyone and the guests looked on. We were placed at a table close to them, with the bride's father, another reason that made us feel special. Geoff was highly amused by another tradition at an Italian wedding. Any guest is allowed to stand up at any point during the celebration, hold up their glass and shout '*i sposi*' which roughly translated means, 'to the bride and groom'. Every time it happened, all the guests immediately followed suit, stood up, took a sip of wine and shouted, '*i sposi!*' I know the English toast the bride and groom, but usually just the once. The Italian way is to give many people the chance to stand up and shout the toast, so it can happen up to twenty or more times.

We set up Emily's wedding in the same way, with a table just for Emily and Daryl facing all their guests. We borrowed an open sided marquee from the town council, which when it arrived, was really old, with a few rips in it and very grubby. I tried to clean it but it was huge. I thought Emily would be horrified, but her reaction was the opposite. 'I love it Mum. It's exactly right for a country wedding. Perfect. It will look so good with the bench seats and the trestle tables that the Comune are lending us.' Talk about a wedding on a shoe string.

Geoff just about managed to get the farmhouse looking good. I had put in bougainvillea and jasmine plants at the base of the wooden pillars around the portico; by June they were looking perfect and the scent was powerful. Emily laid out the tables with white paper table cloths and she used empty tin cans for the table flowers. She had a cheese cake: I mean, a proper cheese cake made out of cheeses. The bottom one was a huge round Asiago, which they had to weigh on the meat scales in the supermarket when we bought it because it was so heavy. On top of that went another three cheeses with a small square blue cheese on the top. It was decorated with cherries and olive leaves and it was certainly different. Daryl and Emily used one of your chef's knives to cut into it.

Emily's wedding was a brilliant affair, but if I'm honest with you, I've forgotten a lot of it. It was the fourth wedding we'd been to that year. The Italian one was first. Then we attended the wedding of Geoff's niece in Northern Ireland. That was hard for me. Mainly because they were around your age and during the reception everyone tried to make me get up and dance but I couldn't do it. Laughing, letting myself go and having fun wasn't just difficult, it was impossible. When I looked at the young men on the dance floor, messing about, joking, having fun, I kept thinking that you should be on there too. You should be enjoying yourself with these young people. At one point I just had to leave the room and find somewhere away from everyone where I could have a bloody good cry and shout, 'Fuck, fuck, fuck. It's not fair, why did it happen? Why aren't you still in the world with us?' I gathered myself up and found the strength to get back into the room and then I did dance — after a fashion. I think I drank enough to numb the emotions for a while. It was still early days in the grieving process and I still hadn't accepted what had happed.

Another wedding that year was ours, Geoff and I. When I realised in Portugal that Laure was not legally your next of kin, I felt she definitely should have been in that position. It made me think about the situation that Geoff and I were in, should anything happen to either of us. When everything in life is going smoothly, it doesn't occur to people what complications might arise after they die. I wanted to make sure that Geoff would be responsible for me and that I would be responsible for him, if either of us should be unlucky enough to meet our end. Even close families can turn on each other after a death occurs. It didn't happen in your case; we involved Laure at every single stage and would not have done otherwise. Geoff and I hastily made the arrangements for our marriage, and we didn't tell anyone, not one member of the family that we were doing it. I remembered what you told me on Skype once when I said that Geoff and I thought we might get married one day but I couldn't face all the hoohah that went with these occasions: who to ask, reception, presents, all that stuff. You said, 'Mum, just do it, go and get married and then tell everyone you've done it.' So, we took your advice.

We simply needed the piece of paper to give us legal rights, it wasn't going to change the way we felt about each other. I know some people think as soon as you get married love goes out of the window but that was not the case for us. We've now been together sixteen years and married for ten, and our love and relationship has grown stronger. Ha! I expect you find that very cheesy.

We had to have two witnesses so Geoff asked Maurizia

the local town police woman. 'Maurizia would you do me the honour of being my witness when I marry Ninette next week, and would you wear your uniform please?' She slapped him on the shoulder and laughed, and she agreed to do just that, as though it was a perfectly normal request. I asked my friend Silvia to be my witness; she worked in the mayor's office, which was where we got married. We weren't able to shut the door to the little room, as you're officially not allowed to marry without allowing the public to enter, consequently, an office girl came in and one of the Comune officials also appeared and proceeded to photograph the whole event. The ceremony was conducted entirely in Italian and we just had to say *si* once each. It was bloody hilarious. At the end I wasn't really sure to whom or about what I had said *si*, but they gave us a certificate in Italian and English so it must be legal. After many handshakes and congratulations from the mayor and his assistants, we went across the street to the Tre Archi bar where we had arranged to meet a couple of friends for a glass of Prosecco and in Geoff's case a Crodino (a non-alcoholic beverage). We walked in and told them we'd just got married, much laughter and congratulations followed. We texted our children and told them what we'd done. They were all a bit slow to react. Joe said something like, 'Congratulations you sneaky buggers'. Matt was out to dinner and drunkenly phoned us. He shouted out to the guests around his table in Singapore and I could hear everyone cheer. Geoff's girls were pleased for their dad. I don't remember how Emily and Wills responded, I think they took the longest. There was no big celebration, but we had dinner with a few close friends that evening at a local *Agriturismo*. I think it would have suited you, running an *Agriturismo*; a self-sufficient bed and breakfast where all the food produced must be grown or raised on your own land or sourced from within a few kilometres of your property. Usually, they specialise in a particular aspect of food. The one we went to for our wedding breakfast, bred their own pigs and produced a huge variety of cured meats. Their homemade breads were delicious: olive bread, walnut bread, cheese bread are just examples. I could imagine you in the role of proprietor, cooking the food and mingling with your guests. Not quite sure where you would have fitted in the graffiti, maybe on the hand-written menus.

I find it hard to cope with the swell of emotions that tear through my body when I know that you are missing out on so many things. As the years go by it should be easier but it's still hard. A great deal has happened in this family since you've been gone: births, deaths, marriages. Instead of the burden of loss becoming lighter over time, it often feels heavier. Like Sisyphus pushing that damn boulder up the hill, the scenario is never ending. I know you will never feel the warm sun on your back, swim in the warm sea, mess around in fresh new snow, hold your baby in your arms, be a grandfather and so many other things; the list gets longer and longer as each year comes and goes. The pain sticks in my gullet like a pebble in a pheasant's crop. I know that I must focus on what you did achieve, and not what you didn't have time to complete. It's bloody hard sometimes though.

New Year's Eve 2011 was spent in Italy. I should have been glad to see the back of that year but somehow letting it go was difficult. A step further away from you. But to survive as a bereaved parent you have to keep going. One small step at a time. Not just for the rest of the family but for yourself. I've never been a fan of New Year's Eve.

It's always a bloody let down. I offered the apartment in our town house in Petritoli as a raffle prize to The Compassionate Friends, a group for bereaved parents, which I had recently joined. The people who won the prize came to stay that new year. The family had lost their son: he had died in February, on the 14th, exactly one month after you. He had suffered from lung cancer and was a very brave young man, only twenty years old. He never smoked and I believe the illness struck him hard and fast. He loved music and the trumpet in particular. 'I want people to listen to the trumpet again,' he told his mum. He played the piano too. He had hoped to go to university in Brighton to study but it soon became evident that he would not be able to continue playing the trumpet or indeed move far from home. He did manage to go to uni in Leeds, which meant he could stay at home and he met a girl in the last year of his life, and lived as full a life as possible. It was different for you as you had no idea that you would be leaving so soon. Would you have done things differently if you had?

Geoff and I and the other family felt the same trepidation that year. We were preparing to face a new year without one of our children.

We were invited to go to some friends of ours just outside Petritoli, who knew the situation and understood how we were feeling. We had a great meal, one that you would have asked a lot of questions about. A tasty beef casserole with plenty of wine and vegetables added, it was scrumptious. I took along an aubergine bake, hardly exciting but easy, which is how I like to cook. There was also a chicken dish, equally yummy, and for the starters or antipasti as they call it in Italy, there were lots of cold meats, some smoked salmon, olives, cheeses and bread.

At midnight we all stood on the balcony watching

across the valley as fireworks were sent up from towns and villages. It was an impressive display but each one stabbed me in a different way. A rocket flying up into the dark sky so bright and full of life and energy, then at its end, tumbling to the ground, a crumpled mess. Other fireworks bursting into bright white lights, red sparks, blue, yellow, green, all wonderful colours, but so short lived. Not enough time to appreciate the beauty of their being. It was all over far too soon. So much energy, so quickly dissipated. I couldn't help but compare your life to the display. Two-thousand and twelve was with us and I would have to face the first anniversary of you leaving us in just fourteen days.

Love Mum xx

Chapter Sixteen

21st January 2021

Dear Tosh,

Today began as a sunny but chilly day. We walked a short route with Jpeg, just to oil the joints in my knees and hips. They were complaining about all the rocky paths and mini canyons they had to negotiate yesterday. Getting older is no fun. You won't have to worry about that, 'forever twenty-seven' that's you. You joined the 27 Club, which I had never heard of before Emily told me, but it's a group of celebrities who all died aged twenty-seven. Kurt Cobain, Janis Joplin, Amy Winehouse — she joined the same year as you but a little later, in July — Brian Jones, Jimi Hendrix, Jim Morrison, and I suspect a lot more. The 27 Club are mostly musicians; we think they must have needed a painter and a cook to join them. You can hold your head up as a musician and singer too. You are in good company and you are a celebrity in my eyes. It's all these little things that keep my chin lifted. You didn't just leave us, you left us so that you could join that 27 Club, not quite unique but special.

Remembering you as a young healthy twenty-seven-year-old is a good mechanism for coping with your loss.

I have watched my children grow each year from birth, until they are all now older than I was when I brought them into the world. Except for you. That statistic will never happen. I know that looking at you as a four-year-old, I couldn't imagine you as a ten-year-old or a teenager. My last memories of you are as a young, handsome man, troubled in some ways, but generally coping with life. In love and thinking about a future. I will never know what that future would have been. I can make it up and have done, but realistically, you will stay twenty-seven for me, and everyone else who knew you. It's the same with actors and celebrities, you remember them as they were in the films and then it's a terrible shock when you see them aged ninety-two or something. Clint Eastwood for example; we saw him on the TV the other night and I couldn't believe how haggard he looked. I mean, you just expect him to look the same as he did in *A Fistful of Dollars* but there he is, all wrinkly and dry. You'll never be old, you'll never feel pain again, you'll never need to wear incontinence pads or become forgetful, smelly and annoying. I will be all those things, so not only will you not have to experience your own old age you won't have to experience mine either. Is that awful of me? To write these things to you? I love you just as much as ever and miss you with a fierce pain , but I have to get through these days, and one way to do that is by having a sense of humour and a sense of perspective. I cannot change what has happened. Remembering you as you were when you left, gives me some small pleasure. I don't have to think of you as old, toothless and grumpy, because that will never happen.

In October last year I was seventy. It occurred to me that when I reach eighty, had you still been with us, you would have been forty-seven. I cannot imagine you at forty-seven. Grandma lived to be ninety-one and if I'm careful I will manage to get at least close to that age. When I look back ten years at all that has happened and imagine how much will happen in the next ten years it's terrifying. Not least because those last ten years have, in many ways, rushed by. It's odd now that I can look back and know for certain that I have lived well over half my life. You will never be able to do that. By the time you were fourteen you had already lived half your life. That thought is both sad and scary. Think how many children there are in the world who have already lived half their lives and they don't know it. I've obviously been living too long with Geoff, who can never think or discuss any subject without bringing statistics into it! It is interesting though, it's only the old people who can say for certain that they have now lived well over half their lives. Uncle David died in September 2018 and my poor sister is now on her own. He was in his seventies so a reasonable time living, although today, seventy is considered young to die. He had a massive heart attack and died at home suddenly. It was tragic but we all want to go that way. We don't want some protracted illness, lying in bed for weeks even months waiting. I suppose I could tell myself that was a good thing for you, but the theory doesn't work because I just don't want you to have died at all. I can only use it if I say, 'Well if he had to die it was a good thing he went quickly'. That sounds callous, sorry. I think you know what I'm getting at though. When the family were all in the hospital, we certainly wanted you to live. It was only afterwards, that we realised that with your brain injury being so grave, death was the best outcome.

Love you.
Mum xx

Chapter Seventeen

22nd January 2021

Dear Tosh,

A couple of weeks ago, during the Christmas break — I say break but with the lockdown situation, everything continues in the same vein most of the time — we went to a socially distanced, mini, classical concert with my odd socks friend and her husband here in the village. We sat outside in beautiful gardens and listened to him play the cello and sing. Live classical music always makes me feel emotional. He played an eclectic choice of pieces, Mahler, a couple of carols mixed with some modern hit songs and ballads. It finished all too soon, the cold affected his fingers so that he could only play for half-an-hour. It made me feel wonderful and sad at the same time. I wished so much that the family could have been here with us to experience it. I filmed a couple of short sections of the concert and sent them to the family on email. I missed my family and thought of you throughout the evening.

This Christmas we didn't see any of the family except on FaceTime and Zoom. We were never planning Christmas Day together but I had hoped they would all visit France at some point during our stay, but that possibility is looking less likely as the days of Covid and lockdown go on. I don't mind so much being home just with Geoff. I'm getting older now so we like to have a quiet time. We used to have some wonderful family Christmases. When you boys were little and belief was still solid in your minds. I suppose Christmas brings back all those memories of you as a little boy, with a smack to my heart every year.

'Father Christmas…where are YOU? Are you UP THERE? Come down NOW.' That's what you shouted up the chimney one Christmas when you were about four or five years old. I've always remembered it, you were so sweet and so earnest, innocent, loved and cherished. The twins, Joe and Wills would have been around two, Matthew and Emily were at home for Christmas. We had a big extended family with you boys being uncles when you were born, me being a step-grandmother and numerous half and step relations. We had some brilliant Christmas days and Boxing days. Very typically English and we were lucky to live in a big Victorian house in the Devon countryside and to have family in Buckinghamshire with an equally spacious house where we could all gather together for family and festive occasions.

Your childhood was truly wonderful, and you didn't want for anything. There was a big garden, grounds and fields in which to play. You climbed trees, built tree houses, raced bikes and home-made go-karts down the steep drive. To be honest I am amazed you three boys survived all the knocks and bumps. The doctor's surgery in South Molton and the A&E in Barnstaple knew us well!

We had nanny Jo to help look after us all; She came to

us when you were a baby and stayed with us on and off for years. She moved with us from Buckinghamshire to Devon and lived as one of the family. We were all fond of Jo who now has a family of her own. She was like a second mother in the house; she and I never argued about anything and we brought you all up between us with no jealousy. You were two-and-a-half years old when the twins were born and I told you they were called Joseph and William. Every day after that you proudly announced, 'This is Jo's Eff and this is my William', pointing at them or hugging them in turn. So sweet.

Before you left, you and I hadn't spent Christmas together for probably five years. You, Joe and Wills came to Geoff's house in Little Chalfont, I cooked lunch and you relaxed. Geoff let you do anything you wanted to do, drink beer, watch TV, put your feet up; there was no pressure on any of you. You all loved it. Not sure what you made of Geoff but he felt an empathy towards you, as he could see himself in you. I think it was that Christmas that he decided to try and help you as much as he could, get you onto a path that would lead you somewhere. He detected that you had low self- esteem, shouldn't really drink as it made you into someone you weren't and that you had dabbled in a little too much wacky baccy and other substances which I don't even want to think about. I'm quite sure he took you on one side and had a chat or two. I believe you had some respect for what he had to say. You knew that previously he had alcohol issues but that he had given up years before. Not drinking had changed his life for the better and he wanted you to see that.

The first Christmas without you, at the end of 2011, Geoff and I spent in Italy and a couple of friends came for lunch. I didn't find the day as hard as I thought I would but I did break down a couple of times. It happened when I cooked because I am reminded of you when I am preparing food. I still have your chef's knives. I think some are missing but I use them and it makes me cry. When I cut up the carrots for lunch that Christmas morning, I started counting. Suddenly I realised that I had got to twenty-three and knew I had to cut one of the pieces of carrot into two so that I would have an even number of carrots. It was you and your 'even numbers' thing. I had NEVER bothered about anything like that before. Chop, chop, chop, I had to do it with all the vegetables, counting to make sure they were cut into an even number of pieces. Since then, I always do the even numbers thing when chopping vegetables. Are you sitting on my shoulder or whispering in my ear?

All these thoughts come tumbling through my head constantly, but that evening during the concert of wonderful cello music, brought me to thinking about what a musical family we are. Emily played the piano and the cello, but gave them up after school. Matthew plays guitar, Joe can get some good sounds from a guitar, saxophone and the piano, but I like it best when he plays harmonica. Wills plays guitar, had a go at drums and violin, and amazingly learnt to play piano accordion. He came to visit us in Italy, and we took him to the piano accordion museum in Castelfidardo, where a guide let him play a tune on one of their very expensive instruments. She stood and watched with her mouth open. 'You play well, but you are playing it upside down!' Wills realised it was because he'd learnt from YouTube and had been following the screen as though it was a mirror. We all had a good laugh I can tell you.

You and your siblings are able to pick up any instrument and get a reasonable sound out of it quite quickly. You played clarinet and drums, and when you left us you had bought a trumpet. I remember you played a tune called *Romance* on the clarinet and you never made it squeak once. I was so proud of you. But like most kids, you gave it up. Joe tries with the sax, he wants to play jazz music. Imagine if I had been more of a pushy mum, I might have got you all playing together as some kind of trio. Do I regret that I didn't make you practise more? Could I have been the mother of a talented musical group? I don't think it matters now. I am still the mother of a talented bunch, you're just not famous. I wonder where the trumpet is now? I must find out. Maybe Wills could learn it.

I'm going to bed with thoughts of you playing beautiful music with your brothers.

Love
Mum xx

Chapter Eighteen

23rd January 2021

Dear Tosh,

We woke to blue skies and a howling, bitterly cold wind this morning. I don't have an obsession with the weather, but I'm sure it has an effect on my mood and memories for the day. Today, I was reminded of Exmoor, where the weather was often unpredictable. The wind and rain whipped our faces as we walked over the moors, it was both exhilarating and painful.

We planned a memorial service for you at the end of the month, and before that day, Matthew, Emily, Joe, Wills and I went on a little road trip. First of all, we drove down to Dartmouth and stayed at the Royal Castle Hotel. The holiday house we'd owned in nearby Dittisham had long been sold, but we went to visit the village, wandered around and had a pint in the Ferry Boat Inn down by the river. We talked about crabbing, regattas, and your dad's boat of course. I wasn't very good on that boat. I used to imagine how wonderful it would be to stay overnight on it. It was a big Fisher 25, at least four-berth I think. But actually, I only felt safe when we stayed in the river. As soon as we went out of the estury and into the sea I became terrified. The boat had a big deep keel, which gave it a rolling motion in the waves. I was no sailor. It had to be flat calm for me to relax and even then, I worried all the time. I don't think you were that bothered about boating, you could take it or leave it. We went out a few times as a family, but when your dad got older I didn't think it was safe for him to go out alone with you and the twins. He couldn't see any problem, but I envisaged him falling down on deck and hurting himself. How would you all get back? In the end he agreed to sell the boat. *Seawhip* she was called. Joe painted a picture of her once. I have it somewhere in a box in the attic. None of you showed any interest in sailing when you grew up. That would have disappointed your dad I think. He would much rather you had been in the sea-scouts than scouting for somewhere to paint graffiti. The only time you wore a sailor suit was when you and the twins were pageboys at nanny Jo's wedding. It was a boiling hot day in the summer in Buckinghamshire. You took your duties very seriously, and did everything you were told. Wills followed you around without putting a foot wrong, but Joe did not want to be a pageboy. He was mortified by the whole thing and clung to your dad's leg refusing to go into the church. Your dad tried to persuade him to at least walk up the aisle behind the bride, he even offered him a pound to do it. But, nothing would work. He did get into the farm trailer after the service to go from the church to the reception. We also managed to get some great photographs of the three of you dressed in your sailor outfits, but I think they might have been set up after the event. Your dad was very patient with all of you, far more patient than I was.

We all loved Dittisham so much. We missed your company on that day in 2011. There was a big space where you should have been beside us. But, talking about you and remembering all the good times, I did feel that you were at least in our hearts. During those first few weeks, we became experts in the art of putting on a good face and being jolly. We tried to find happiness in memories and that can be done. Matthew said, 'Just think of all the good things he did Mum. Celebrate the life he had and try not to think about what he's missing now.' I tried, but frankly, that was, and still is, almost impossible. Dittisham equals happy holidays with your dad, me, your siblings and occasionally, with extended family. It seems a lifetime away now — and of course it is.

I haven't been back again to Dittisham since that day but I'm planning to take Geoff soon. I know I'll feel your presence there, but it will be you as a little boy. When I dream of you, it's always as a little boy rarely as an adult. You often pop up in my dreams, and you never die in them. Whatever age you are when you appear, you are always very much alive. I never dream about the accident when I sleep but I do go over it again and again in my head; day dreams I suppose you could say. I try hard not to put myself through that any more. If I feel it coming on I do an activity to distract myself but it has to be an absorbing one like reading a good book or studying some poems. No good just taking the dog for a walk, because I do even more thinking then. Writing all these letters brings back mixed emotions. I have to look at photographs and dig deep into my memory bank, which can often be quite upsetting.

The next place we went to on our little road trip was Landacre Bridge. Exmoor is such a wild and beautiful area. Do you remember how, in the summer, we would pile into the big Peugeot 505 seven-seater car? It was brilliant that car. I could not have managed with anything smaller. We had a succession of three I think. Even with the big car we still had to take two cars when we went away for a weekend.

You all loved going to Landacre and we would take everything with us: buckets and spades, food, swimming things, nets, towels, deckchairs, balls and rackets. You would all paddle in the water, trying to catch tiddlers in your fishing nets and we would picnic on the grass. I used to take a book or magazine, so that I could sit and read while you all played. It was shallow enough for me not to worry and you never ventured far away when you were small. When you were older you would wander further up the river where it was deep enough to swim.

Sometimes, in the winter, we used to drive the forty minutes from our house with the dog, walk up and across the moor, which was always windswept at any time of the year. You kids moaned like anything. What is it about children that they don't like walking? We didn't often see Exmoor ponies, but there was such excitement when we did; watching their soft muzzles searching the scrubby land for grass, hoping that we could get close enough for a quick stroke. Of course we never did, they're wild after all. We got closer to the sheep, which fortunately, Polly, our dog ignored; she was too lazy. The best thing about walks in the winter was getting back home, lighting the fire and having a hot cup of tea.

Lucky children. Landacre was, and still is, the same as it has been for very many years. Only the road might have changed from a stony track to tarmac and now cars drive by rather than walkers or people on horseback as it might have been.

When we were there in 2011 with your ashes, Matthew had the idea that we should do something bizarre. 'Take a handful, and throw them up into the air to land on the water. You must leap up as high as you can, and shout a silly word, or a saying, or something funny,' he said. As an essentially extrovert family it seemed a perfectly natural thing to do. We began with quite normal things like, 'Tosh' or 'Gorf' or 'graffiti' etc., but then we deteriorated fairly rapidly into 'cranberries!' 'sausages!' or 'cabbages!'. All ridiculous words, that you would have appreciated I'm sure if you could have heard us.

The water was so cold that day, I wondered how you children ever managed to swim in it. Mind you, it was January. We left little particles of you in the water at Landacre. I watched them float away and thought of your soul floating somewhere. I really wanted to believe in something after you had gone. It would have suited me to think that you were joining your dad and grandma and other family members, but however much I tried, I couldn't bring myself to accept any of that religious stuff. I'm sure a great many people would be damning me for writing to you like this, but I'm not knocking those who believe; I almost envy them. I'm sure they would also think it dreadful that we split you up and left you in various parts of Europe; Italy and France and England. What difference would it have made if we'd left your ashes all in one place?

I planted a rose bush at the farm in Italy and spread some of your ashes under it, and also in the small olive grove to the side of the house, away from the main plantation. A little piece of you in the countryside and sunshine. We gave some of the ashes to Laure and her parents organised a plot for you in the tiny cemetery in their village in France. You are in a beautiful spot looking out to the north eastern landscape of Lorraine, over the fields, with a wooded hill in the distance. The headstone is made from granite in a modern pyramid shape with a small photograph of you at the top. Geoff and I went to see it when we visited Laure's parents in 2015 on one of our trips back to the UK from Italy. It's truly beautiful and I am so glad that part of you is there. I've just looked at the photographs on my phone and I took seven of the headstone. I deleted one so that now there are six of them; a nice even number.

Sharing you around would appeal to you; you liked fairness. Fairness made you donate to Amnesty International. I'm not sure if you realised this, but Amnesty was also one of the charities your dad subscribed to. He couldn't stand injustice, and always fought for human rights. He never went on marches or did any demonstrating, but he would definitely be defending anything he considered unjust when debating around the dinner table. That makes it sound trite but you were the same; always defending the underdog, the less privileged. Your boss from the catering company told me, that when walking with you through Cardiff you would never ignore anyone destitute sitting on the pavement, but always had a word for them and a spare bit of cash. He said something like, 'It didn't matter to Tom what their background was, or who they were, he would always stop and speak to them'. It's a pity everyone isn't like that.

In the end, when we left Italy, I felt it was right to bring the remainder of your ashes back to England and Bristol, and I'm sure you would approve. We chose the Garden of Remembrance in Arnos Vale Cemetery. Friends and family can visit whenever they wish and just have a few moments silence. The grounds are beautiful and you are surrounded by people of all ages who are all missed and loved. Tiny babies, one-hundred-year-old men and women, and everyone in between. I like to wander around and read the headstones and plaques, and appreciate some of the beautiful stone statues. I have a favourite; a full-size angel who stands not far from you, she is pretty and has a caring face. I know you are in good company.

We organised a plaque, and the final laying of your ashes to coincide with my sixty-fifth birthday in 2015. Geoff and I flew over from Italy, Matthew flew over from Thailand and the whole family had lunch together after spreading your ashes in the Garden of Remembrance and putting the plaque in its place. The plaque reads: 'Thomas Anthony George Hartley, 1983-2011 Do things that make you happy.'

At the end of a video that Matt filmed with you about graffiti, he asks, 'So, what's your final summary?' You pause for a second, smile, and reply, 'Do things that make you happy…' give a gentle laugh then Matt laughs too and says, 'Great'.

That little phrase, 'Do things that make you happy', has become our family motto.

Miss you
Love Mum xx

Chapter Nineteen

24th January 2021

Dear Tosh,

I have felt sad during the period of your anniversary this year, much sadder than I expected to feel. Each year since you left, the graffiti boys — I don't know what else to call them and I don't think there are any girls — from Cardiff and Bristol and for all I know other towns too, get together and paint. They call it the Gorf Jam. They had planned a big one for this year, it being the tenth anniversary, but of course the virus has put an end to that. There's a big lockdown in the UK at the moment. People can only leave their houses for essential shopping and for exercise once a day. Unless they are key workers like Joe who's working in the hospital in Bristol; sometimes he's caring for the patients who have the virus. You have to work from home unless it's impossible to do that. You are also not allowed to meet up with others who are not in your household. I know those involved in the jam are all very disappointed.

Setting aside personal relationships and friends, graffiti was the most important thing in your life. You were well respected and liked by everyone in the graffiti world. 'He painted so much. Unstoppable. He painted in some of the weirdest and most obscure places as well as legal walls and everything in between. Very passionate and driven and brave,' said one of your mates. I dread to think of where those weird places were.

You bought your paints from Oner Signs in Cardiff and hung out there sharing sketches and photos of graffiti with friends that you made from the Cardiff graffiti scene. I know that at one point you were thinking of working there.

The first Gorf Memorial Jam was held in Cardiff on the roof over Oner Signs. Over thirty people turned up to paint for you. I couldn't go because we were in Italy but Joe and Wills were there and so many of your friends. There has been an organised paint every year since you left. I find it difficult to write or say the word *die* or *died*. I prefer to say lost, left, gone, anything but *died*. I look forward to the yearly jam, not that I've ever been, but we usually send beer or money for beer for all those taking part, and they turn up whatever the weather. Afterwards photos are posted on social media and I love looking at who's attended. Since 2017, when they moved back from New York to Bristol, your nieces have also joined in. What kid wouldn't love to get covered in paint? You would so enjoy watching them spraying randomly, or using a stencil to paint your name…TOSH or GORF in big graffiti letters. They love their Uncle Tosh even though they've never met him.

I have an image in my head now of you wearing your hoody with a rucksack on your back. You always carried paint cans, a sketch pad, marker pens and beer. It's the graffiti boys uniform, which you wore and carried with pride. Ten years on and most of the painting you did on walls, railway tracks, disused buildings and parks, is now gone, but we do have photographs. Lots of them. In drawers, boxes, books and on the wall.

I wish so much that you could see the respect and love that is poured out for you every year. It is a bloody wonderful testament to the person you were — most of the time — I have to add that because you weren't that amazing all the time and I don't want all this praise to go to your head. I mustn't let my motherly bias affect what I write to you. You were no saint.

Thinking of all this made me very happy which switched on the guilty button I carry with me everywhere since you died. Losing you has sent me on an emotional roller coaster ride. I know that sounds like a cliché, but that is exactly what it has been from day one. To begin with, I went from numb and unbelieving to destroyed, angry and desperately sad. But there were several occasions, even quite close to when I first lost you, when I would feel happy about a memory, laugh at a joke, get the giggles with Geoff about something ridiculous. But, as soon as these intensely cheerful moments came over me then the guilt button would be triggered. How could I be happy? How could I laugh or find anything funny when I have lost you? I should not be allowed to laugh or have a good time in any way whatsoever. I expect that's what the Victorians thought about bereavement. You had to wear black and be in serious mourning for a number of months or even years. I don't think you would have wanted me to be like that but at the same time I couldn't switch off that guilty feeling. I had no right to enjoy myself ever, about anything. It's not so bad now but there is a little part of me that still says I cannot be fully happy, even after ten years.

Bereavement wasn't new to me. I'd lost my father in 1963, in a car accident, (I've told you about that) then, when I was in my thirties, my best friend died. She was the closest friend I ever had and has never been replaced. Then, in my fifties, first my husband — your dad —died and then my mother two years later. But, when I lost you it was unlike anything I had experienced before. This guilty button could be switched on for a variety of reasons. Part of the guilt I felt when you went was similar to the guilt feelings I had about my dad. I thought I could have prevented your accident, if I had contributed more in supporting you when you were going through troubled times. Maybe, had I been more involved in your recovery then you would not have had a drink that night. You were twenty-seven and had left home ten years previously. Although I didn't love you any less, you were living your own life and I had let you get on with that. When the guilt gets bad I tell myself that had I given any advice you would not have listened to me anyway.

I have a guilty secret that I've carried around for nearly ten years and I have not been able to share it with anyone, not even Geoff. I thought that members of the Compassionate Friends group, and maybe some of our extended family, would consider your death not to be as bad as the death of another son or daughter who had died in a road accident, from cancer or in childbirth. I imagined they might think that I didn't have the right to grieve as much as they did. That you brought it all on yourself. There is a stigma attached to street painting and graffiti. Many people think it's a bad thing to be doing, and they hate it because it is illegal a lot of the time. I have never spoken to anyone about this, and maybe sharing it with you is not a good thing. You could tell me that I'm right, your death was avoidable, but that doesn't help me, that doesn't make my loss any easier. Numerous times I have to answer, when someone asks the question,

'How did he die?' and the reaction I get is sometimes tangible. The person disapproves. I can almost hear them saying, 'Well what do you expect? Mixing with all those gangs. Disfiguring public buildings'. The sympathy is less than it would be had you died of some ghastly illness. They don't actually say it though. Generally, people are not good at saying what is really on their minds. I have told myself, that whatever the reason for a child's death, the grief and loss for the parent is equal in its depth. I wondered today, having at last shared my secret, what it must be like to be the mother of a convicted murderer. A heavy burden to carry, a heavy heart and the guilt must be almost unbearable. Actually, I feel a little less worried about it now I've told you. Sharing and showing emotions is important. I should have talked about it earlier. I shouldn't care what people think and from now on I won't. Other people's opinions will have no bearing on my grief.

I don't want to end this letter on such a downer so I'm going back to the Gorf Jam because even though it couldn't happen the way everyone wanted this year there were some amazing tributes put up on social media. Individual artists painted solo pieces showing RIP Gorf, Tosh, hearts and other images. Evie and Orla painted in the skate park in Bristol. Simon and his two little kids painted on a huge piece of paper in their back garden. I cried, but not in a sad way. I cried from pride and love and the graffiti guilt has somewhat lifted. I may well have given it the boot.

I love you so much.
Mum xx

Chapter Twenty

25th January 2021

Dear Tosh,

Today the temperature was around 8 degrees and breezy. The *Tramontane* wind blows here and it can be a tad unpleasant. The *Tramontane* comes from the north-west and is a dry, pretty violent wind and cold in winter. We've had gusts of up to 60km an hour at times since we've been here. We went for a walk with Jpeg first thing and then later I decided to go for a bike ride with Geoff. We cycled to a convent not far from here. I would have turned for home then, but Geoff decided otherwise, and we carried on to the next town before turning home. When the wind was behind us it was okay but at one point the *Tramontane* was blasting my face and making my eyes water. I had my fingerless mittens on and had to stop and cover my fingers up with the flap before frost bite took hold. In the end we did ten miles which for me was a long ride.

Geoff cycles a great deal these days, more than when you were around. He began when we were in Italy, but when we returned to England to live in Dorset in 2016 he joined a local club and then cycled at least three times a week. I'm not a keen cyclist, and Dorset is a bloody nightmare because there are so many hills, but a few years ago I gave in to Geoff's pleadings and graciously received the gift of an electric bike for no other reason but to make him happy. We took the bikes with us when we went to France for a holiday in 2019 and cycled around the Loire, and I have to admit I enjoyed it. We stayed in Saumur where the countryside is beautiful and flat — and that's the important word, flat — with long quiet roads running alongside the river Loire. It's flat here too, around the town where we are staying so I also enjoyed today. There are a couple of hills, and this morning as we made a steady climb towards home I zapped up the gears and sped off on the electric bike, flew past Geoff and waited at the top of the hill. 'Where did you get to?' I tried not to smirk but my sarcasm fell on deaf ears.

'Top of the hill isn't for another 100 metres,' he said and carried on cycling. I followed him at his pace, it would have been mean to beat him. I'm too soft I think. It was so good to be out in the fresh air, peddling my little legs off. Although they're not so little after Christmas. I have put a few pounds on. Laying down an extra coat for the winter I think.

You might be wondering why I'm telling you all this? It's leading up to explaining the effect that grief had on the physical as well as the mental side of my life. When we got back to Italy at the end of January 2011 I had to go to work and we were living in the townhouse in Petritoli. The farmhouse was really a summer place at the time as you know, because we had only partially renovated it. The townhouse had central heating and modern bathrooms and although we let a large part of it as two holiday apartments, there wasn't much call for them in the winter months. Most days we would go down to the farm to walk the dog and do some essential work on the olives or the garden. We would let the dog out of the car at the top of the farm road and she would run down the two kilometres in front of the car. Geoff encouraged me to walk around the field with her too, he said it would be good for my mental health — which I knew — but it was months before I could be bothered to do any exercise. My body was simply a support for my bones, muscles and organs. I ate without enjoyment and I found it almost impossible to walk any distance. I would struggle down the hill to the bottom of the field by the ravine, and work my way around the edge of our property at a slow trudging pace. My legs were heavy. I literally dragged myself around and it pained my muscles. I swear I was wearing lead boots. It went on for months like this, but I didn't share how I felt with anyone. I did go to the doctor who wanted to put me on anti-depressants. 'I am not depressed,' I said, 'I'm grieving, can't you understand that?' I wanted Valium and he was reluctant to give me any. He didn't know me well enough to realise that I would probably keep them in the cupboard and only take one when desperate. It's easy for me to write that now, but I suppose he could have been right. Even so, anti-depressants were definitely not the right route for me. I just needed time. You almost have to let your body indulge in the grieving process to get you through.

Strangely, I didn't 'let myself go' as Grandma would have put it. I went regularly to the hairdresser and tried to keep myself looking — to outsiders — as though I was in complete control of everything. I didn't shed tears in public and I didn't spend all day in my dressing gown and I didn't resort to drinking too much alcohol. I did have a drink or two and I probably got drunk a couple of times but I didn't turn to drink. I just had a problem being enthusiastic about anything. Walking, swimming, riding a bike, basically anything that required energy I could not be bothered with. It was too hard for me. It was as though I had become lazy. I did my teaching job and I think I was pretty upbeat in the lessons. Nobody could imagine the turmoil that went on inside. I smiled at people. I just got through each day on automatic pilot mode. I don't remember exactly when things began to change but I felt like it for some years. It was odd for someone like me who loved dancing to find that I was unable to enjoy the rush of blood to the head and the tingling that buzzes through my body when I dance to a piece of music that I love. You know exactly what I mean because I think you enjoyed that adrenaline buzz too, except you transferred your buzz to street painting. I tried yoga and meditation but that didn't work for me. I think, when you are in the depths of despair and your heart aches beyond anything you have ever experienced before, then you have to give yourself time.

A couple of years after we returned to Dorset I joined some writing workshops and through a woman I met at a poetry meeting, I joined a Laban Dance Group. All the members were over fifty — I think — and the teacher was inspiring. She managed to cajole all of us into 'losing ourselves' in the music. It was so unlike the dance I had taught, which had been ballet, tap, modern all with structure. That's not to say that the Laban is a free for all do-what-you-like method, but it is based on human movement. Three components: direction, weight and speed. This, combined with the eight efforts: wring, press, flick, dab, glide, float, punch and slash. I loved it. My body loved it and I could lose myself in the music or in the words that the teacher said to us as we created and choreographed on our own, with partners and with groups. I now miss this class so much. I wasn't able to attend in 2019 because I took it upon myself to do an MA in Creative Writing at Exeter University and my seminars fell on the same day and time as the Laban class. After that the pandemic came to stay and no dance classes were allowed. There was a small window of opportunity which I was unable to take before lockdown stopped the classes again. When I dance it can make happy emotions swell, my heart beats faster and, boy it feels good at the end of a two-hour session.

Another new friend made me have another go at yoga and this time I quite enjoyed it. Didn't stick at it though because it began at nine in the morning and for me that's just too hard. I could have managed it when I was younger but now, I have to walk the dog before I go anywhere, so that means a really early start if I'm going to be ready to attend class by nine. But, I have to tell you about one experience I had. At the end of one session we did something they call a 'mantra'. The teacher spoke as we went through the positions of the exercise, breathing and pausing all the time. I felt a huge well of emotion rise inside me and all I could think about was you and I just cried. When we'd finished I explained to the teacher what had happened and she asked, 'Have you lost someone?' There must be something to this yoga lark eh? Not sure it will ever become a habit with me though.

Namaste
Love
Mum xxx

Chapter Twenty-One

26th January 2021

Dear Tosh,

When I got up from my bed this morning and walked through to my workroom I was astonished to see that it was snowing. Bloody snowing in the South of France! This is not what we came here for. Whatever the weather Jpeg needs a walk. We dragged on some warm clothing and pulled our woollen hats down over our ears. I don't mind wearing the face mask — required by law in France because of the virus — when the weather is chilly because it helps to protect my red nose. This affliction is something I've inherited from Grandma, a little rosacea, which makes me look a bit of a lush sometimes. The skin specialist in Italy said there wasn't much I could do about it, but I should avoid spicy foods, too much alcohol and not expose my nose to extreme cold or sun. All this seemed impossible. I love a good curry and it is always tempting to sit in the sun, I like a drink and the weather in England is often cold. The doctor's English wasn't good so, to explain one remedy for sitting in the sun, he cut out a little triangle shape from a piece of white paper on his desk and stuck it over his nose, suggesting I should do this when sunbathing. Ha bloody ha. I thanked him, paid my money and left.

It was pretty this morning; little flurries of snow that tickled as they fell on my cheeks. Snow equals kids having fun. Snowmen, tobogganing, snowball fights, freezing wet hands. Soggy clothing and boots left in the hallway, coats dripping water as they sit on the banisters; all followed by hot drinks and painful toes in front of the fire. Memories of Elwell House again. The driveway was a whizz for flying down on bum sledges or bigger plastic sledges. I remember you racing down to the gate and trudging back up again. That's the problem with sledging, the trudging back up the hill. We were lucky we didn't need to go anywhere in the car to find hills. The field behind our house was steep, but sometimes the horses were in it, which meant no kids racing around. I've never been keen on the winter, but snow is the best thing about it. Always fun to play in the snow, especially when it's a bright sunny day, but then, lovely to come in from the cold and warm up.

When you were about nine and the twins seven, we went to stay with our friends the Leishmans in Switzerland. Peter Leishman always called you boys, Tom Boy, Willy Bob and Joey. It was quite endearing when you were all little but wore off when you were in your teens. It was the first foreign holiday for the twins, first time on an aeroplane for them and only the second for you; you had flown once before, to Canada when you were only eighteen months old. That had been to visit the Leishmans too, when they lived there. There wasn't a lot of snow around in Switzerland. It was April and by that time, most years, it's thawing on the lower slopes, and spring well on the way. I love Switzerland, the Alps, the valleys, the cheese, the cows and the scenery is reminiscent of *Heidi* the children's story. You must know it? The house that Peter and Sandra rented was a chalet on the side of a hill. I swear I could hear goats baaing and alpenhorns blowing in the distance every evening; there were certainly plenty of cowbells. It was *Heidi* land.

The Leishmans were determined to get us to ski even though the snow was light. They knew all the places that we could get to with enough depth to allow us to 'have a go'. Your dad was close to eighty years old at the time, so we parked in the car park at the bottom of the slopes. Took the lift up to the top and left him in the café with a big mug of coffee. I hadn't reached fifty yet, but I had never skied before and I hadn't realised they had taken us to a red slope, which I now know is not for beginners, but at the time it meant nothing to me. We were all kitted out: boots, skis, anoraks, warm trousers, and off we went. Peter, I think, gave you a quick lesson and then sent you off. Then he and Sandra took it in turns to take the twins down the slope between their legs. You boys all took to skiing without any problem and were soon managing very well to fly down the run. For me it was a different story. I'd been given the basics of how to stop and turn, and I set off cautiously. I was absolutely useless. I don't know why, but I hated it every time I gathered any kind of speed. It took me the best part of half an hour to get down once. The minute I felt the skis begin to move any faster than walking pace I panicked, couldn't remember how to stop so just threw myself on the ground. Then I would have to struggle up and try gently moving again. All the while I was going down, you and the twins would pass me.

'All right Mum? Great isn't it?'

'Well done Mum, come on.'

'You can do it Mummy, don't give up!'

Every bloody time you lot passed me — which must have been at least ten times — you made comments. Laughing and smiling, happy little boys.

When I eventually got to the bottom and took the lift back up to the café my hands were numb, my bum was sore and my head thumping. I'm not prone to headaches but I got a corker that day. I sat down with your dad.

'I am never, ever going to do that again. It was awful. I can't do it. Maybe it's the dancer in me, I don't like having to keep my knees bent, and turn my toes in and…' I went on and on.

'Those boys did well didn't they? I managed to see them go off each time from the top. They were all doing it by themselves by the end. I suppose the centre of gravity for them is a lot lower than yours which might have made it easier. Never mind, darling, you tried.' I could have smacked him honestly, but my head hurt too much.

You took easily to athletic pursuits being fit and agile and with a good sense of balance. Your skating and skateboarding techniques were good, and you would practise over and over again. Isn't human nature wonderful? Anything that we want to be good at we can work and work at it and never get bored. If only you had approached your academic work in the same way as you approached skating and graffiti. Sorry, it's only natural for a mother to think this way and to blame themselves saying, 'I should have been stricter with his/her school work'.

Writing to you about our Swiss holiday has reminded me of the visit to the Leishmans' house on the lake in Canada. You were only eighteen months old, when we went in the summer of 1985. We flew on a jumbo jet,

131

which was full to capacity. Matthew and Emily were sent to the very back of the plane to sit by themselves. I felt awful for them because we were so far away down the front of the plane. I expect they thought it was fantastic, being unsupervised for several hours, with the aeroplane attendants rushing about after them. Your dad, you and I were seated near the first class dividing partition, where there was a bassinet to pull down in front of me, for you to sleep in. Bit of a joke, I don't think you slept a wink. You definitely did not sleep on the flight back to the UK, because I remember as we touched down at Gatwick you completely crashed out and I had to carry — what felt like a ten-ton dead animal — through the corridors, escalators and lifts of Gatwick; nothing woke you.

We flew to Ottowa where Sandra met us and drove us to the small town of Portland, where we parked up near the water. We transferred everything into a little open boat with an outboard engine. We had to squash our luggage, Sandra's shopping, other supplies and the four of us into — what appeared to me something you might row around a boating lake for fun; it felt overloaded and just a tad dangerous.

'We'll have you there in no time. Peter's waiting for you, the kids are so excited to see Uncle Gerald and meet Matthew and Emily. Paddington the dog, is looking forward to it too…' Sandra was, and is a great talker and she has the most wonderful, theatrical accent, speaking perfect Queen's English.

As we pushed away from the shore, the weather began to turn nasty, and the lake became very choppy. Matthew and Emily loved it but I was a bit scared. I think your dad was fine. Having spent all that time in the Navy a little bit of rough water wasn't going to upset him. You loved it, bouncing around all over the place. I had a life jacket for you (which we'd bought to use on your dad's boat in Dittisham) and I must have dragged it out of one of the bags and fastened it on you. Sandra had a couple of life jackets for Matthew and Emily but the adults had to make do.

'Don't worry, Gerald, don't panic Ninette, it will be fine. Just a little squall, nothing for you to worry about.' Sandra stood at the tiller like Flora MacDonald heading for the safety of Skye and she saved us all!

The cottage — as they call it incongruously — was a fairly large property even then, four bedrooms I believe. It was not finished when we visited all those years ago; now it is surely magnificent, although I've not been back since. It didn't bother me too much that it was incomplete, but I must admit, no proper lock on the bathroom door was a bit worrying with four adults and seven kids living in the place!

The weather only stayed bad for that one night. Next morning, we walked out of the cottage into the grounds. We were surrounded by tall trees, tracks through the forest and pathways down to the private pebble beaches, and the dock by the lake. There was no barrier between the land and the water, nothing to stop a toddler from falling off the edge of the dock and into the crystal waters. I ran after you as you raced away to discover your new surroundings with the sure- footedness of an excited eighteen-month old — in other words — tripping over tree roots that were pushing up from under the ground, hauling yourself up and rushing on towards the water where you obviously saw no danger. It was then I decided to put on the life jacket and leave it on for the rest of our holiday.

I wish I could have given you a metaphorical life jacket to take to Portugal.

Peter was a bit gung ho about the way I followed you around and protected you from falling into the deep waters of the lake. 'Let him fall in Nin, he'll either float or swim…he won't go down, believe me. We've done it with all our kids.' But I didn't believe him.

When you were just over a year old, your dad wanted to take me on the QE2. I had never been into boats and cruising but he had taken several cruise holidays with his first wife, Hazel and had enjoyed it immensely.

'We'll just take a short one, we'll get underway from Southampton and it will be five days out and back. You'll love it.'

'Will we have to go through the Bay of Biscay? I don't fancy that at all. I'll be scared.'

'The QE2 has massive stabilisers, you won't feel a thing. Anyway, it's not always rough in the Bay.'

I eventually agreed that we would go. We had to take you, so a cabin with two beds and a cot between them was booked. I had imagined a suite with a magnificent vista to the sea through a large window. As it was we didn't even have a porthole. Inside cabin on a lower deck. The noise of the engines was a constant thrum. But, I didn't complain, the QE2 was a beautiful ship, a floating luxury hotel. We were able to dine out in the evening because we could organise a babysitter. I became quite excited once on board, and looked forward to the ship moving away from the quay and heading into the night. However, there was a problem with the propeller; sailing was delayed, so we had a romantic dinner looking out over Southampton Docks. We crept back into our cabin feeling tired and full of food. You were sleeping in your cot as we got into our beds around midnight.

By six o'clock you were awake. We tried to ignore you but you stood up, peered over the edge of your cot and began talking gibberish to us. There was nothing for it but to get up, go on deck and have a stroll around. It was just about daylight and to our surprise we were still in bloody Southampton!

Later that day the boat set sail. I took you along to the day nursery so that you could play with the other little children and your dad and I could have some time to relax, shop, look around the ship and see what was on offer. Unfortunately, you didn't like the nursery. You howled and made such a fuss. Guided by the lovely staff, I left you anyway, thinking you would settle when I was out of sight. When I returned after an hour you were still screaming. I hadn't the heart to abandon you, consequently the whole of that very short sea voyage passed without a single break from our one-year-old boy. Except after you had crashed out in the cabin in the evenings.

My most fond memory of that trip was of you on the dance floor of the QE2. Early in the evening there was a fancy-dress competition for the children on board. I bought a multi-pack of mini boxes of smarties, emptied them all out and then stuck the packets onto some big plastic pants that I used to put over your nappy at night. You wore them with a vest top and I made a banner with the word 'smartypants' written on it. I didn't expect you to get any prizes but what happened was so cute. The band were playing before the party really began, people were sitting around, drinking and relaxing and you walked right out onto the dance floor and began moving and dancing to the music. The audience loved you and began clapping. Nobody joined you and I wasn't asked to remove you from the floor. You were amazing, even the band leader turned around to watch you. Great natural rhythm and style and at that age no inhibitions. Your dad and I were so proud. The next day when we walked around on deck people kept smiling and calling out to you, 'Hello smartypants'. It was the highlight of my holiday.

I should just add that your dad was quite right about the Bay of Biscay. As we sat eating our lunch on the day we passed through it I could not feel a single wave but he said, 'Look out at the horizon Ninette. See how it's going up and down.' I stared out of the window and I could see a considerable amount of rising and falling occurring in the distant sea line. 'You see? The stabilisers are doing their work. Here, have another glass of wine, that'll make the decks wobble for you.'

We didn't have that many holidays abroad. We couldn't afford them when you were young. The recession of the late 80s and early 90s hit us badly and we made a few wrong decisions with buying and selling houses and the dance magazine lost a lot of money. We could no longer holiday in Dittisham as we'd had to sell the house and the boat. All at a very bad time unfortunately. The year after that, we sold Elwell House and moved to South Molton, which gave us a little bit of money in the bank. Your dad insisted that we spent it on a fly-cruise at Christmas. Grandma was in hospital in Weston Super Mare, having had a massive stroke and I felt awful leaving her, but your dad was adamant.

'I want to go on a cruise and I want the boys to come. We've not had a holiday for a long time and it will be a wonderful experience for them. An education. I will not take no for an answer.' He turned his back on me and went into his study where he proceeded to book it all up at a cost of around £4,000, which was a lot of money then. I had no desire to go on a bloody cruise but I had no choice.

I spent ages making a calendar for Grandma and wrote several cards which I put in envelopes, to be opened each day while we were away, which I think was around ten days; I left them with the staff at the hospital, who were kind enough to take care of it all for me. We didn't have smart phones in those days, no Skype or video messaging like there is today. I was worried about leaving her without much support. It was December 1998 and she'd had her stroke at the beginning of October.

Our cruise was a total disaster. You were so badly behaved. You were a stereotypical teenager, fifteen to be precise but you were the epitome of — can't-be-bothered-with-any-of-this-shit, boy; miserable, uncooperative, unhelpful, annoying...there aren't enough words to describe how awful you were. I'm sure, in later years, when you looked back you would have been ashamed, but I look back now and laugh at how ridiculous the whole situation was. You barely spoke a word for the duration of the holiday. You never smiled and just hated everything. Thank goodness the twins didn't mind it, in fact they loved it. It was an 'all inclusive' cruise which meant you could eat all day long if you wanted, and I think the twins did. They went from the breakfast buffet to lunch buffet taking only an hour in between. They ate afternoon tea, then we all had dinner every evening. We only had to pay extra for alcohol, which you were all too young to have. It wasn't just because of you that the holiday was bad, but it was also because, although it was still early days, the dementia your dad was suffering from became more evident away from his home environment. He got lost on the ship all the time, which meant I could not let him out of my sight. He fell over more than once, because the ship's stairs and gangways were narrow and difficult to negotiate. Christmas lunch was ghastly. I remember trying to jolly everyone along and feeling like a referee at a toddler's party. Glaring at you boys to behave and trying to pretend that everything was hunky-dory.

I can't remember many of the stops the ship made but I do recall stopping off at Agadir in North Africa and we had organised a camel ride for everyone. The expression on your face as you sat on that camel is tattooed in my brain. There's a saying, 'if looks could kill' and you certainly knew how to communicate that! We also stopped at Madeira and walked around the town of Funchal. It was here that your dad had one of his falls on the steep cobbled narrow streets. Getting old is no fun, but coupled with dementia, it is very much harder. He was excited to show you some of the places he'd visited before, and to tell you as much as he could about the history of the towns and countries. None of you were that interested; you were all the wrong ages. You, Tosh, couldn't even be bothered to feign interest. I think Joe and Wills made an effort.

We never went on any other family holidays and as we lived in a beautiful part of the country, we didn't feel the need to go away. In North Devon, we had Exmoor to walk on and the coast at Braunton, Saunton Sands, and Putsborough to visit. I have some wonderful photographs taken on the beach at Westward Ho! when you boys, and your dad's grown up children and his grandchildren from his first marriage, came to visit. The tide is out and the beach stretches a long way. I'm sitting on the big boulders watching you all play cricket. The extended family is large; all your nieces and nephews older than you. How strange that must have seemed. I know it's confusing to people who don't know us. Emily has given up with relationships in our family now and she just calls all of them cousins.

I don't think you boys missed out too much by not having any further holidays abroad.

I love you Tosh, even though you were a massive worry to me.

I miss you.

Love
Mum xx

Chapter Twenty-Two

27th January 2021

Dear Tosh,

On our walk this morning, Geoff and I were talking about the day of your memorial service in Bristol. He had gone back to Italy but then flew to London the day before the service and stayed with his friend in St. Margaret's, Twickenham. They then drove to Bristol in the morning, collecting Jackie and Lottie on the way. Geoff didn't get to see that much of his girls when we were in Italy. It was a shame that the reason for seeing them this time was such a sad occasion. I can't remember how the rest of us got to Bristol. I do remember worrying about what to wear. Stupid isn't it? I didn't want to wear black but I didn't want to wear anything outrageous. I settled for a long grey linen skirt and a multi-coloured top of muted oranges, greens and greys, with a smart jacket over the top. I hadn't got any suitable shoes and a good friend lent me a pair of expensive, black suede ankle boots that were a bit tight.

I am so proud of everything you managed to achieve. Your memorial service was a real celebration of your life. There was crying of course, but some laughter and I could see so much love for you soaring over everyone's head, reaching out from those smiles and tears. All your close and extended family came, and many other relatives and friends arrived to pay their respects. You were remembered with much love and warmth. It wasn't a happy day but strangely, it wasn't sad either. I have a feeling I'd saved one of those tablets they'd given me back in the hospital in Porto, and I took one of them before arriving at Arnos Vale Cemetery.

We'd left Matthew to organise everything with the celebrant. Everyone crammed into the Anglican Chapel, a beautiful and serene building. It didn't have to be used as a place of religious worship, and we based your service on humanism. The celebrant did give time for everyone to have their own thoughts; religious or otherwise. We had selected music to be played throughout the service. Laure chose 'While You Were Sleeping' by Elvis Perkins. I hadn't heard of it but she said you loved it. He wrote it for his mother after 9/11 when she was killed in one of the aircraft that crashed into the Twin Towers. I can't listen to it now without crying but sometimes I play it because it makes me feel better to have a good weep now and then. It's a kind of crazy self-inflicted emotional torture. I think it has something to do with bottling things up, which is never good; it's a release of sorts.

Simon Banbury made us laugh when he talked about your two-man gang, 'The Hurty Boys'. He explained: 'We said that we would make short men put on dresses, we'd push over prams, and spit at pigeons. We didn't of course, we just went shoe shopping'. He finished with a quote from a song by The Jam called 'Thick as Thieves', which included this line: 'We'd stick together for all time, and we meant it, but it turns out just for a while'. I was so touched by his obvious love for you. More than friendship, there was also loyalty, like another brother.

I wanted to speak and I was pleased that I didn't break down, but I couldn't tell you anything about it now. I can't remember any thoughts or emotions. Matthew said a few words and Laure had written a beautiful speech which Joe read for her. It would make you blush, her genuine love was overwhelming; I re-read it the other day and the emotion of loss came rushing back to me. She said so many beautiful things. She spoke of your generosity, your kindness, your love, but also of your anxieties and problems, but my favourite bit is this: 'Tosh was passionate. He was not afraid to love too much in a world that dictates indifference and selfishness. Tosh transcended the banality of daily life and appreciated the smallest things: being warm at home on a rainy day, waking up by my side, sharing a piece of cake on a sunny afternoon. On our last Sunday, I cooked him some crepes, spread them with my mum's jam and gave them to him. It made him as happy as if I had told him that the STR crew would put up a piece in his honour. Tosh had a distinctive ability to see the magic in everyday life.' She ended her speech with: 'I will always be thankful for the richness, love and intensity he brought to my life.'

It hurts to read all these eulogies but I'm so glad to be able to look at them again. The pain of reading them also brings comfort. What a lovely girl Laure is. You were so lucky to have had that relationship. I know that since you left, I have imagined that your life with Laure would have been idyllic. Living in France maybe with a couple of gorgeous children. Laure with an academic career and you being the house husband. I believe you told me once that's what you planned, and when Geoff and I were old and doddery you would take care of us in a big house in

France. Not sure who's going to take that on now! Of course, it's easy for me to make your life perfect and I try not to kid myself that it would have been all roses for you. You would be pleased that Laure has moved on, I know you would.

I absolutely loved Emily's contribution to the ceremony. She read out some emails that you and she had exchanged from past years. I particularly liked this bit: *No, I don't have a girlfriend yet but hopefully I will bump into a pretty girl on the way home from the market and knock all of her groceries on the floor and help her pick them up, and like in the films I will be round her house helping put her olives, stuffed with sun dried tomatoes and feta into her fridge before we realise the chemistry that is happening between us.* You had a great imagination. I'm not sure I appreciated how talented you were.

I wish I could remember all the lovely things that were said at the ceremony and all the people I met for the first time; from your world of work and from the graffiti world. I had met your mate Rhys Evans before; he spoke well of you, but I don't have a record of what he said. What I do recall is that he spoke about his son. Rhys said that it showed how much he thought of you because he had absolute faith in leaving you with his child to babysit. I believe he said, 'I wouldn't leave my boy with anyone that I didn't totally trust'.

I was amazed how many people turned up who knew you through street painting. You were really well known and respected in the world of graffiti. Incredible. Of course, I was aware that you, Wills and possibly Joe did graffiti but I had no idea the extent to which you had gone with it. I'm afraid I'm a complete numpty when it comes to graffiti and now I wish so much that I had taken it all more seriously. When you boys were just kids I was in complete denial about the graffiti in the park by some artist called Coner. It turned out to be Wills! Unbelievable. Joe tells me he only dabbled in it but then he was hell bent on causing trouble in other ways. He was the one brought home by the police on two occasions. Once for throwing a water-filled balloon at a car and once for letting off a fire extinguisher. I thought *you* were the good boy.

Not far from The Paintworks, the graffiti crews and some individuals from Bristol, Joe, Wills and Simon and other friends from all over, gathered together, either the night before or very early in the morning of the 27th January. I think they were led by Will Horner — Emily's old boyfriend and your good mate — he came over from Australia for the ceremony. Will was the one who first introduced you to graffiti. When he and Emily were at university in Exeter they often used to come to Elwell House. You and the twins spent a lot of time with Will and I think that the fascination for graffiti began right from day one. Will was an inspirational painter and photographer. You were a natural. He and the others did you proud on the day of your memorial service. They painted a massive piece for you. They used the name Tosh not Gorf or Fiber and it was the most fantastic tribute. I think almost everyone who attended that day, at some point during the afternoon, walked down to view it. I'm no good at measurements, but I can assure you it was bloody massive. Shades of magenta, pink and white with outlines and writing in black. *Tosh RIP. Tosh we will miss you.* I absolutely loved it and wanted to hug everyone who contributed. I'm not sure I thanked them enough at the time. It was such a fitting piece of artwork for you. The shame of it is, that it has gone the way of all graffiti;

painted over. Maybe one day, in thousands of years, it will be discovered by future archaeologists as they peel away the layers looking for evidence of the past. At least we have loads of photographs that can be shared, or hung on a wall. I've even used it as wallpaper on my computer.

The tributes didn't finish there. Another was painted in a street near the city centre a few days later. The police arrived to move the painters along, but they were told what was happening and why they were painting, and the police left them all to get on with it. Then when Emily, Daryl and Will got back to Australia they painted a tribute for you at a big legal site near Bondi Beach. I'm pretty sure that it's gone on like that ever since. Tributes to Gorf, Tosh and Fiber, popping up all over the place.

We had business size cards printed that Will Horner designed, with a photograph of you on one side and an inscription on the other. I had seen the Italians make these little cards. I liked the idea that we could hand them out at the celebration of your life, for people to have as a keepsake. I carry mine with me everywhere: it's in my purse, and even though it's laminated it's looking a bit worn at the edges now. Emotions were high at The Paintworks that day; it was filled with love, brotherhood, camaraderie and real admiration for you.

It was a long and stressful day. My feet were sore from my too tight boots, and I couldn't wait to get back to the hotel. We did have a choice of which hotel to book into in Bristol, but it seemed fitting that we would choose the Ibis. Back at the bloody Ibis. The hotel of tears, laughter, bad food, hysteria, phone calls, decisions, flight bookings, cremation and funeral arrangements; the Ibis saw it all. We even considered meeting as a family every year at an Ibis, but we didn't. Only Matthew sent the family a text on one of your anniversaries, *I'm having a drink in the Ibis Bangkok and raising a glass to Tosh*.

The day after the service of remembrance, we all gradually made our way home to our respective houses and countries. To describe the memorial day as a 'high' wouldn't be quite right, but I think, up to that point, I had been coasting along on making all the arrangements for your final goodbye, contacting friends — there was a constant stream of things to do. When it was over, the real world came crashing back down around me. Back to a life where you no longer existed. A new phase on my own journey through the years. Whereas previously I had remained, to a certain extent, buoyed up with the necessity of making arrangements and dealing with things, I now felt heavy and defeated. But 'life goes on' as they say. I pushed forward in the best way that I could manage, but without you anywhere.

I miss you so much still.

Lots of love
Mum xx

A HERO IN THEIR EYES

To see a scar on some young chest and know
that inside pumps the heart of my design
would give me some idea, and maybe show
me the reason why   you had to die

As a baby, I felt your heart beat strong,
then after twenty-seven years   I listen
while life ebbs, and finger tips hang on.
I hear the rhythm of the lung machine
Let me go, let me go it pumps as we
debate   then sign the forms for them to take
important body parts.   They really need
to operate   before   you   deteriorate.

You were a hero to six families
But for your own   this is still agony

Chapter Twenty-Three

28th January 2021

Dear Tosh,

It was the most wonderful sunny day today. So warm that we sat in the garden to drink our coffee and talked about this and that, mulling over things, and considering what we have to be grateful for. Geoff and I always say our lives are good. We do both know however, that 100% happiness can never be mine again. Losing you I lost a part of me that can never be replaced. Even though I have days of joy and spend time laughing and appreciating life and living — like the warmth of the sun in France today — every second there is a little cloud hanging around that I can't quite shift.

On this day in 2011 I received an email from Doctor Eduarda Pereira from the hospital in Portugal. It read:

> *Hello Ninette,*
> *I'd like to let you know that Thomas will forever be a hero for 6 different families. On their behalf I would like to thank you for your selflessness and*

generosity in allowing Thomas to literally save the
lives of their sons and daughter.

Once again thank you and I hope this news
allows you and Thomas' loved ones to find closure
and peace.

Eduarda.

I cried so much when I read those words for the first time, and I have cried many times on re-reading them. It is a beautiful email; if the adjective beautiful can be assigned to the medium of email. A handwritten letter or card would have carried more poignancy. Those days are long gone, even a typed letter is unusual these days. But, I'm not bitter about it, just sad. Portugal took all the corporeal parts of you, the whole of you, the 'being' of you. They took everything they could use and left the family with nothing. This aspect of your death is the hardest part that I have had to come to terms with, and frankly, I'm only just beginning to appreciate the good side of it.

I want to be glad for those sons and a daughter, happy for their parents, siblings and families, and be thankful that our loss, your death, meant that others could live, but it is hard to comprehend that those parts of your body that I made, are now functioning in some other being, a stranger to you and to us. It is the most difficult thing for me to imagine.

I wonder would it help if I met the recipients? Did the little girl take your heart? I see myself talking with her, looking at the scar and maybe even placing my hand on her body to feel the beating of your heart. How old was she? Let's say five, that would make her fifteen now. She might have been older, and now in her twenties, even twenty-seven or older. Your heart and other organs have

149

already lived ten years longer than you did. Your heart is now thirty-seven. How bizarre is that?

I wasn't told what organs they took and so today I looked up which ones they might have been. In 2011 they could take up to eight organs: heart, liver, kidneys x2, pancreas, lungs x2, and intestines. If they took all those then I'm guessing that someone had lungs and heart, another the liver, another pancreas, two people for kidneys and a different person for intestines. That makes six altogether. In 2014, in the UK they brought in a law to say that you could now donate hands and face. I don't think I could have coped with that. It's just too much like science fiction, plus, the thought of someone walking about with your features would be unbearable — I can hardly believe I've written that — it is surreal. But at the same time, the suffering for some people must have been relieved because of this law. I'm thinking of those who have experienced bomb blasts and terrible burns to their faces.

I think, perhaps I would like to meet the person who has your heart, but I'm not interested in seeing the recipients of other parts that were taken. The heart was the very core of you. The heart begins to beat when an embryo is only twenty-two days old in the womb. Incredible. I don't imagine I ever will meet this person, I wouldn't know how to even begin to discover who they are. Besides, in the worst case scenario, it might not have worked and how might I feel then? Bereaved all over again. I expect other mothers feel the same as I do.

I'm sure I shouldn't dwell on this, but it occurs to me that you could be all over the world by now. We took your ashes and spread them in many locations, hence they are in Italy, France and England. You are a well-travelled dead person — that was my attempt at making a joke. You could be living as far away as Australia or America. Somehow, I hope not. I would like to think of you in Portugal surrounded by smiling happy people. Your heart beating in someone else's chest. A steady throb that can quicken when love comes knocking. A heart that is the essence of a life, for a vibrant, singing, laughing young person who is content with his/her life. Perhaps they are good at art and music. I hope your heart beats for them until they're eighty or more.

Our family has a strong sense of humour and that is what got us all through and still gets us through each day, but the organ donation is something that I cannot really jest about even though, as you can see, I've tried. I cannot get it out of my head that you might have been able to feel something when they operated. I thought I had got over that anxiety now but reading up about it today, I saw there was a medical paper that suggested brain dead people might feel some pain, during the procedure of transplant; a rise in their pulse rate can occur. I told you, that at the time, I asked the doctor, and she assured me you would know nothing. I have to believe her. I wish they had let me go through to the operating theatre to be with you when they switched off the equipment that was keeping all those vital organs working. There are many things that I wish, but the only way to get through, and survive losing you is to put one foot in front of the other and move forward every day, even if it's only a little bit.

A hero in the eyes of six families. That is wonderful. You should be so proud. I am certainly proud, even if that pride is tinged with anger and sadness. It is no compensation for losing you but it does go some way to making your death seem less of a waste. Writing this has helped me to come to terms a little with the organ donation, however painful. I do hope the person who has your heart is as compassionate as you were.

I love you Tosh. I miss you.
Love Mum xx

Chapter Twenty-Four

29th January 2021

Dear Tosh,

I hope you didn't mind too much having such an old dad. It was occasionally amusing. I remember once a man gave a talk at your primary school about World War Two. Afterwards he said that it went very well except one little boy kept insisting that his dad had been in the navy during the war! The teacher said, 'Oh, that'll be Thomas.'

Whenever people think of you as a boy they remember the dancing. You could do a brilliant Michael Jackson impression. Hat tilted on your head, jeans and a T-shirt. I have a DVD of you dancing to 'I'm Bad', your moon walk is perfect. Natural rhythm and pretty good co-ordination. You fought the academic side of life. You found writing and reading difficult and your dad insisted on taking you to an expert on dyslexia. I wasn't convinced but went along with his wishes and accompanied you when you went for an interview. He asked what it was like when you tried to read and you said, 'The words all jump about on the page'. I didn't believe you. That's bad isn't it? But I thought you'd heard other people saying this. The man tried lots of different coloured lenses in some weird frames and in the end, he decided that you needed blue ones. Most of the time they were to be found in the bottom of your school bag; afraid of being teased you very rarely wore them.

Sport took up a bigger role than the academic side. Although team sports, rugby or football were not for you. It could have had something to do with the sports masters at school. You opted for basketball, judo and — this is the odd one — chess. That began at Filleigh primary school where Julie Carder encouraged you and you ended up with a little metal badge that said 'Chess Captain' or something similar. There's a great programme on Netflix at the moment, *Queen's Gambit* all about chess, obviously. I haven't played for a long time but thinking, probably like the rest of the Netflix watching world, of taking it up again and teaching Geoff. Your dad played chess. It must have been him who originally taught you. I played with my friend Vee from Weston Super Mare, she taught me when I was in my early thirties. I was laughing about it when watching *Queen's Gambit* because they talk about all the different moves made by certain famous players. Conventions, I think they are called, the same as in bridge. Vee and I once went into the chess club in town, and were horrified when people asked us questions like, 'Is that move 18... a6!! from Spassky vs Petrosian 1966, Game 7?' Don't ask me what it means, I just googled that particular quote, but you get the idea. We hadn't a clue. Our laughter rolled around the back streets of Weston as we walked home and we never went back to that club again.

You must have felt like that with your reading sometimes. As though it was all gobbledygook and the words on the page intimidating. When you were a very small boy you proudly said, 'Look Mummy, I can read the whole book without looking at the words'. It was a book about frogs and you read every page with your eyes closed. I ought to have realised then that there was something wrong with your ability to read but not with your memory. Another clue to your struggle was when I realised that you were unable to recognise your own name on a jar of Hartley's jam. After that, I spoke to Mrs Hardwick, your year two teacher at Filleigh Primary school, and she was the one to get you reading. She took you on your own every morning before assembly and worked slowly, until you began to recognise the shapes of the letters and words. I should have paid more attention to your reading problems. Here I am, beating myself up again for being a bad mother. Did we even play chess together? Your chess days were very much a short-lived thing; perhaps in the prep department of West Buckland School you might have played but not by the time you were a teenager at South Molton. Then, you were into all the 'naughty boy' stuff. Skateboarding, drinking and dope smoking. I'm not sure when the graffiti began but you never had a problem with drawing the words and letters by that stage. I hope it hasn't taken you too long to read this letter. At least it's not handwritten, you don't have to decipher my very messy script!

I don't think a day has passed without thoughts of you, but this year, this month of January, you are on my mind more than ever. I see young men, who I guess might be your age, and I still feel angry that you're not here.

It's raining today and I have been writing and cake baking. I cannot cook a single thing without you in my mind. I don't know how much of a baker you were, but Emily told me last week that you baked a mean banana bread. What I do know is that you loved to eat the cookies and cakes I made. Having three young boys at home I can remember several occasions when I would cook a batch of biscuits in the morning, put them in the larder and by the afternoon they would be gone. Once, I wrote on a piece of paper, *have you asked if you can have one of these?* I put it in the tin on top of the chocolate chip cookies. About five minutes afterwards, one of you shouted up the stairs, 'Mum, can I have one of those biscuits please?' We had a good laugh about that. I sometimes miss those times. All of you at home in that big house.

You and the twins built a tree house. Emily was horrified when she discovered from Joe the other week that your dad let you boys make a tree house using proper tools: a saw, an axe, a hammer and nails. Not a toy spanner or plastic saw in sight. I never thought anything of it. It didn't occur to me that it might be dangerous, although I might have drawn the line at any power tools, a chain saw for example. Luckily, I don't think we had any of those. As far as I remember there were never any major incidents, just the occasional splinter. Nothing was ever broken and not much blood spilt. It was a good tree house made from anything you could find. I think you were about ten and the twins eight. I never worried about you playing outside. You were lucky children to have the freedom you did.

You were all into making go-carts out of wheels and wooden boards that you found. Or converting anything that already had wheels into some kind of contraption that you could race with. Other boys would come and play from the village. I don't know what their parents must have thought when they went home with tales of the Hartley boys building dangerously fast racing boxes. There was a steep, curved driveway, about fifty metres long and you boys would race down it crashing through the open gateway at the entrance. It's a miracle that nobody was seriously injured. I'm surprised you children didn't end up in hospital more often. You were *all* bloody reckless and fearless.

You were reckless in January 2011, weren't you?

Mad boy…miss you,
Love Mum xx

YOUR CHEF'S KNIVES

The bag smells   not of you
but of musty food   the knives
are sleeping   bound by narrow straps
        last tied by you

Your name drawn by you
on the outside of the canvas
in blue indelible ink
        a tag of sorts

As I cut the carrots I count
ten slices   are   eleven pieces
eleven slices   for   twelve
        you, and even numbers

The day they were delivered
you cut your finger   deep
it was the paring knife
        you couldn't help playing

First day as a chef wearing
a bandage   our laughter
carved channels in our cheeks
        you should have waited

The bag is dirty, the knives
are not sharp   my hand
on the handle touches you

Chapter Twenty-Five

30th January 2021

Dear Tosh,

Geoff and I walked 7km with the dog today. It was mostly flat, but it was also a mistake. We didn't start out with the intention of walking that far but we were well over half-way round our route when I put my hand in my pocket and discovered I had lost my glasses.

'Why did you take them off?' Geoff raised an eyebrow. 'Why not put them somewhere safer than a pocket that you keep dragging your phone from?'

I thought he was a bit harsh.

'I'm really sorry. It must have been when I looked at the phone to see how far we'd already walked, or to take a photo, or to reply to Emily's message.'

'So, just the three possibilities then?'

'Yes…or maybe four, because I also had to have a wee, remember?'

'We'd better retrace our steps.'

So that's what we did. The second area we investigated was where I'd stepped to the side of the track, into the undergrowth to have a secret pee. We scoured the long grass, but the glasses weren't there. Geoff began to laugh.

'What is it?'

'Are you sure you only did a pee?'

'Yes. Why?'

'What's this then?'

He pointed at what looked like a little poo in the grass. On closer inspection, we saw that it was a frankfurter that some vineyard worker must have dropped from his packed lunch. We started laughing, the kind of laughing that turns into giggles and you can't stop. It felt so good to let go for a short while. It's good to know that nowadays I can sometimes laugh as much as I did before I lost you. It is possible to take myself away from the sadness, which is particularly prevalent at this time of year. Today when I laughed, I wasn't guilty about feeling happy for a moment, because I know that you would have joined in the laughing had you been there.

I remember so many times that we laughed together. It is good for the soul to have a belly laugh. There's a photograph on a window ledge back in Dorset. It's of you, Wills and me, in Cardiff I believe and we are all laughing. It's very animated. I remember the occasion well and to begin with we were just pretending to laugh, but of course it rapidly turned into the real thing. Emily sent me a similar photograph this week, with her, you and Wills, also in Cardiff, in your flat; in that one you are all throwing your heads back with mouth open except for Emily who is covering her face. She obviously couldn't control herself. I wonder who the joke was on? As a family we have always laughed a lot, especially at ourselves. Nobody was ever allowed to get away with a stupid action without someone sending them up about it.

I'm thinking now of the time when you bought your chef's knives. You began work with the catering company as a pot boy, doing the washing up, and you were slowly promoted to better things. You weren't that bothered about climbing the catering ladder. Your interest in graffiti was at the forefront of your mind, and I guess that job allowed you the time to do it. You could dream up plans for pieces of work in your head while you scrubbed the pans.

Your immediate boss encouraged you to take things further. He told us at your memorial service that he thought you were quick to learn and nothing was too much trouble. 'I thought he could go far if he put his mind to it. He was a great guy and good to work with. I shall really miss him,' he said. He was right, you were too intelligent to stay washing the dishes for long, but you were in good company; after all George Orwell spent a fair bit of time as a *plongeur* in a hotel in Paris, cleaning up after everyone.

When, eventually, you began training to be a chef you were told that you had to buy a set of knives. They were very expensive, and they arrived in a canvas roll. You couldn't resist opening them to just 'have a go'. What a disaster that was. You cut your finger so deeply that you had to go to A&E and get it stitched. I would love to have been a fly on the wall as you told the nurse what had happened. It must have been hard to face them all at work the next day, with a big bandage wrapped around your hand. Fortunately, your superb upbringing had taught you always to laugh at yourself for doing something silly. I know that as soon as I realised the damage wasn't too serious, I found the whole incident hilarious. We laughed together about it on the phone. Sadly, I have never been able to laugh about the last time you did something stupid. The consequences were too drastic. Had you survived and been one hundred percent whole again, then we might, eventually, have laughed the whole thing off. How wonderful that would have been.

I cannot believe that January 2021 is nearly over. 2020 was a difficult year with the virus taking hold and the first month of this year has been a strange one. I had actually been looking forward to celebrating your life on the tenth anniversary of your death, but it didn't pan out the way I wanted it. I should have been able to indulge myself in conversations about you. Meet up with people from the Compassionate Friends whose sons and daughters have recently had a ten-year anniversary. I wanted to see vast swathes of graffiti posted on walls and underpasses in Bristol and for social media to be buzzing with your name and affirmations of friendship and 'We'll never forget Tosh' plastered all over social media. There was some action of course but nothing like as much as I had hoped there would be. Now, the month is almost over and it's too late. It won't be the same celebrating in 2022, it will be eleven years, and I know how much you hate odd numbers.

Geoff and I will be returning to England and Dorset at the end of March. When we get back to England I want to visit Arnos Vale as soon as restrictions allow, and put some flowers beside your plaque. I'm also going to book into the tattoo parlour and get that second tattoo done. I need to focus on doing something positive and concrete to commemorate your tenth anniversary before 2021 is over.

Sometimes Tosh, however bad things are in your life, you have to look around and be grateful. Back in 2011 I was lucky to have a loving extended family with room to accommodate all of us, and give us support for the few weeks following your accident. We all piled into Geoff and Anthea's house in Bucks, and were looked after. We spent our time making sure that all relations and friends knew what had happened, and informing the authorities, such as the bank and building society of your accident. Making plans and sorting out paperwork, all these extraneous activities kept us busy. Matthew had set up a Just Giving Page to raise funds for BASIC (Brain And Spinal Injury Centre). He did it while we were still in Portugal and looking for things to do to pass the time in the Ibis. That makes it sound as though it wasn't important, but as soon as we had the idea we became enthusiastic, emailing everyone we could think of who might make a contribution.

Immediately after we knew how devastating your prognosis was, and we had accepted that you were brain dead, we discussed the situation and realised that we were grateful that you had not survived. Does that make sense to you? We felt that particular scenario might have been worse for everyone. You would have hated being in a wheelchair, unable to care for yourself, and in a permanently vegetative state. Matthew told us, that he had already decided to give up his job and take care of you if that's what was needed, but I was honestly glad that it didn't come to that. We threw ourselves into raising the money for BASIC and managed to raise £3,060 from friends and family. It felt so very good.

I read a wonderful book written by Cathy Rentzenbrink, called, *Act of Love*. Her brother was sixteen when an accident left him in a persistent vegetative state. Cathy's family cared for him for years. But eventually decided the best thing to do was to get permission to let him go, by withdrawing food and water. It was a harrowing experience. When I think about how that could have happened to you, and to our family, I am thankful that you died instantly.

It's really late now, and I'm thinking about you and those knives, and all the other silly things we laughed about over the years, and I'm reminded of another incident that really showed me what sort of boy you were. One year for Christmas, I think you were about ten, and you were give a huge Lego space ship set. It took you all day to make it and the control and patience you displayed while building it was extraordinary, but that's not the end of the story. When it was finished, you stood up and looked around for somewhere to leave it. Deciding to take it to your bedroom you bent down to pick it up and as you walked through the door it caught on the edge causing you to drop it. Everyone held their breath as they looked at the broken space ship.

'Oh dear,' you said, calmly picking up the pieces, and set about fixing it.

Gosh I miss your laughing face.

I'll write again soon.
Love Mum xx

THIS PATH I DID NOT CHOOSE

I didn't choose this path I walk,
my steps are pulled from heavy sludge
the cliffs each side are scarred with
cries of mothers whose weaving treads
I'm forced to follow, our boughs torn
off and lost inside a blue miasma.
I didn't choose this path I walk,
my other branches need support
the one I've lost can't be repaired
but we hold onto memories and try to live.
I didn't choose this path I walk,
but as I learn to navigate, a little way ahead
I see his smile, a light to urge me on,
along this path I did not choose to walk

Chapter Twenty-Six

31st January 2021

Dear Tosh,

Today is the last day of January, and as with other years, from tomorrow, the weight of your loss begins to lift for a few months. From November one year to February the next year is hard going for me. All those events to be remembered: my father's death 28th November 1963, your birthday 30th November 1983, your death 14th January 2011, my mother's death 18th January 2005 and finally, your father's death 1st February 2003.

The first few days in Italy, after we returned from England, were difficult. The Italians are more open and tactile with their sympathy. They're not afraid to hold a hand, hug you and speak words of kindness and love. They care about the person who has left, they care about the ones left behind. It has a great deal to do with religion and praying, but I didn't mind that. It's their way and I was grateful for the words of comfort. A family who lived at the top of the farm road, lost their fifteen-year-old son in a moped accident in 2009. Do you remember it happening? The mother was distraught and the whole town turned out to mourn at the funeral. He was such a friendly lad. He used to ride down to our farm on his dirt bike, come racing in through the open gate and straight across the grass in front of the house.

'Hey,' Geoff had shouted in his limited Italian, 'We don't mind you riding in, but stick to the field.' Matteo gave the biggest grin, waved to us, promised not to come too close to the house again. After that day he often popped down, brought us some wild asparagus, joked with Geoff, asked lots of questions about England. He was so full of energy and life it was hard to take it in when he died. His mother's outpouring of grief was intense and overwhelming. I had no idea at the time how deeply distressing the loss of a child is, but I know now. His mother went to the cemetery twice a day and every day; she took flowers and wept.

'He was only fifteen Ninette. He never even had a girlfriend. He never had the chance to love a woman. There is so much that he was unable to do. He was just a boy.' She sobbed, her whole body wracked with heartache. I know everyone's reaction to loss is different and I can say that when I did cry for you, I mostly did it alone. I'm not good at weeping in public, which might have made some people think I was hard or not as upset as I should have been. It must be my upbringing. Believe me, when I experienced bereavement as a mother, I then understood how Matteo's mum had felt. I admired her ability to let herself go and weep. She may well still go every day to the cemetery.

I'm not good at handling people who want to show too much sympathy either. When someone else starts crying and is unable to cope I don't know what to say. About a month after my return to Italy I met up with a friend for coffee and we talked through what had happened to you. I expect I was still feeling a bit of denial, but she was a counsellor (not mine) and I went through the events with her. I was okay, I guess it helped me to talk about it but she was a wreck. She cried the whole time. I had a bit of a joke with her about it so we were cool. Maybe it's a natural reaction of mine to keep it together when other people lose it? Perhaps I should be a counsellor?

When we got back to Italy at the end of January, Geoff had to go Germany with a friend. He had promised to help him with some building work on a house he owned there. Quite a few people disagreed with Geoff leaving me at that time, but I wasn't bothered. Geoff was very good with me, he knew exactly when to leave me alone and when to comfort. I never wanted too much comforting. Like I said, I cannot stand anyone being overly kind or too sympathetic, I like to be alone in my sorrow. Geoff left for Germany, and I was by myself in Italy with the dog. I had accepted a job working as a mother tongue teacher of English at a primary school in Macerata, a town about a forty-minute drive from our home. The children were age four to about nine years old. I had to travel three times a week to teach little children, who didn't want to learn, how to speak English. Mostly I played games with them, sang songs, or did colouring. I had my TEFL Certificate but it was very basic. The authorities just wanted to know if I had a degree, which I did but it was in Dance Education. They didn't care, they just liked the *madre lingua* mother tongue English Lady. For most of that term, for each drive to and from the school, I bawled my eyes out. At one point as I turned off one main road onto another, there was a large carpark beside the dual carriageway, and on it was one of those small square concrete buildings, housing electrics or something. On the side of it there was some graffiti sprayed and I swear it said GORF. It couldn't have done of course, it must have been something else but the first time I saw it I read it as GORF, and my heart jumped and I began to cry. I got used to seeing it though and after a while I began to wave at it each day as I passed.

There was no staffroom at the school and not enough time for me to drive home at lunchtime so I used to sit in the car, eat a sandwich and cry again. I bought a dongle for my computer. Do you know what that is? It's an Internet stick so that you can get onto the web when you're not on the WIFI. I plugged it in and then browsed the internet looking for anything about bereaved parents. It was at that time that I found the website for the Compassionate Friends. For me, it was a harbour of friendly people who were all a bit lost and needed somewhere to pull in and moor up for one night, or in some cases many years. I signed up and looked through the forums.

Each day there would be new people logging on and new threads to follow. I didn't feel alone in my grief anymore and by that I don't mean that I was lonely or nobody cared about me; obviously family and friends and especially Geoff cared a great deal, but they didn't understand what it was like to lose a child. They could appreciate the loss but they couldn't really 'get it'. Here I found so many people who shared the same fears and anxieties, grief and appalling helplessness. There were stories of parents who had lost their only child, or some who had lost more than one son or daughter, leaving them childless. Dreadful scenarios of siblings killing siblings, and many drug related suicides or children ending their lives because of bullying. Daughters dying in childbirth because of the incompetence of the hospital. Honestly, the stories were endless, and I knew then, that my story, though my worst nightmare, was definitely less horrific than others.

In the months following your departure, as with any death, there was a ton of paperwork. It began with the permission to donate your organs, then the death certificate and a certificate to bring your ashes home to England. There were also the council tax people to deal with who kept on sending demands for money even though we told them you were no longer able to pay, the reason being that you were dead. Dealing with the flat in Cardiff was a nightmare. You were letting it, and had been advised by the agent to take out an insurance in case the tenants failed to pay their rent for any reason, which was good. But, there was no life insurance and no mortgage protection insurance. I could not believe that the Santander had given you a mortgage without insisting that you had some kind of insurance to cover the mortgage. Money could never compensate for your loss, but it would have been so much easier if we could have kept the flat in Cardiff for Joe and Wills. It was a lesson learnt too late. The mortgage company wouldn't allow me to take over the mortgage; it was impossible for Joe and Wills to take it over, Joe wasn't employed at the time, he was student. It was just a mess. I'm not blaming you, it wasn't your fault at all, someone should have advised you. It was down to others, including your mortgage adviser or Geoff or me. We had lent you the money for the deposit and we should have made sure our investment was secured. This is making it sound like I care about the money. I seriously don't. It was just one of the things that added to the burden of your loss. Fuelling emotions of *itsnotfair* and *noneofthisisright*. I don't care about it anymore, but I did at the time. Eventually, the flat was repossessed and sold, but not before we went back and salvaged the furniture. I was not going to allow the stupid mortgage company to have any more than the absolute basics. We stored the stuff in a lock-up in Cardiff until Joe rented a place in Bristol, and then he used it.

My grief is not as acute as it was in 2011, but it has never completely lifted and I don't suppose it ever will. Grief is a journey on a path that has no ending, it just leads on ad infinitum. I have learned to accept living without you, but I will never forget you. The melancholy is always hovering. Sometimes it rears up to spend a few hours or days with me before I pack it away. But it's like a jack-in-the-box and the slightest thing will have it leaping out at me again; a photograph, something someone says, or a baby born to one of your friends. It could be the weather: sun, rain, fog or snow. The smell of cooked breakfast or coffee brewing, or someone smoking weed, or the same tobacco as you. There are, and will be, constant reminders. That might not be a bad thing. Today, it's Sunday and I walked on my own, with Jpeg. We saw a magnificent rainbow and I just thought, 'I wish Tosh were here to see this'.

Missing you as ever.
Love Mum xxx

Chapter Twenty-Seven

1st February 2021

Dear Tosh,

This year, spending time in France, and writing to you, has brought me some solace. I have spent every day with you, which has been wonderful. This morning I walked the dog on my own while Geoff went for a long bike ride. There was blue sky around, no wind (for a change) and as I walked I thought about you. I tried to focus on all the love, humour and pleasure, your life brought to me, to your family and to your many friends.

Eighteen years ago, on this day, your father died. It was a hard time for us as a family. I suppose I always knew that he would die before me, at least it would have been a secure bet at the bookies that he would go first. He was an intelligent well-read man and it was a cruel blow for him to be diagnosed with dementia. To wake up every day and not know where you are or what's happening to you. His life had been long and interesting. A private investigator since the age of sixteen, first working for other agencies and then running his own, King's Investigation Bureau, for over fifty years. He never spoke much about his work, preferring to say he was in 'security' which led most people to believe he had a fleet of security vans. He never bothered to advise them otherwise. He lived through two world wars. Although he would have not been aware of the first one, he served in the second until invalided out with concussion. He always said he was given a second life when meeting me and being a father to you and the twins. I think we all made him happy.

Dementia is a horrible illness. I kept your dad at home for as long as I could, but it became more and more difficult. It was hard living with him at that stage. I had to keep the front door locked because he would wander off into South Molton. Once, the local newsagents called me to tell me he was there. He had no money, and still had his pyjamas on under his coat. It broke my heart, because when I went to collect him and bring him home I discovered he had gone out to try and find a birthday card for me. It was so sad because it was actually around the time of my birthday. Another time he became very agitated and angry with me, telling me I was not to go out into the street because 'they'd be looking for me'. It was something to do with his work, a job he'd been on in the past that he was convinced he was still working on. I tried as much as I could to keep things hidden from you and the twins but you were aware of how bad he was and I think just tried to keep out of the way. I know I was constantly saying the words, 'Don't do that, you'll upset your father,' or 'Be quiet! Your dad has just settled down'. It got to the point where he was spending twenty-four hours a day in the bedroom. Fortunately, it was large with an en-suite bathroom. But, I couldn't tie him up so inevitably he would wander around the house in a confused state. Often, not knowing who anyone was or what was going on. The moments of lucidness became less and less. He took to his bed on many occasions and just wouldn't budge. When it became really bad I called the doctor who came to assess him. Geoff and Anthea attended, we all sat around the kitchen table and discussed what to do. It was suggested that he should go into the community hospital in South Molton, at least to give the family a break for a while.

It was a lovely hospital, and some of the nurses there had children who attended the dancing school, so they knew me and your dad. I remember that first night in the house without him so clearly. You, Joe and Wills behaved really badly; you were noisy and running about the house, playing loud music and fighting on the stairs. You had been released after months of living in a restricted atmosphere, so I couldn't blame you. I felt relieved too but then the phone rang. It was the hospital: 'Mrs Hartley, you'll have to come up and help us. We can't settle your husband into bed and we need you to speak to him.' I went that night and for a few nights after that too until a week later, the staff said they would not be able to keep him there. They couldn't cope with him. He needed to go into the secure unit at the hospital in Barnstaple where they had specialist staff who would be able to assess his needs and decide what the next move would be.

I know you didn't like visiting him in the secure unit. The twins went a few times and Joe even took Polly in on the bus once or twice; the hospital didn't seem to mind the dog visiting. I went every day to see him. It was hard, because they told me that he would never be well enough to come home, but it was impossible for me to explain that to him. In one of his lucid moments he asked, 'How long do I have to stay in here?'

'It's just while they decide what's wrong with you and

the best way to proceed with treatment,' I answered as honestly as I could.

'Well they better bloody-well hurry up because they're all mad in here and I will be soon.' He was making a bit of a joke of the situation. Heart breaking.

After just a few weeks of hospitalisation he became bedridden. He just lay there and didn't do anything, he was fading away. He didn't speak or respond to my touch. I found not knowing how long he would be in this state difficult to deal with. I asked the sister on the ward, 'How long will my husband linger like this?'

'It could be days or weeks, we just don't know.' She leaned in towards me and asked, 'Do you come every day to see him?'

'Yes, I do.'

'Sometimes they don't want to let go. They're worried about those they're leaving behind. Why don't you go in now and tell him that you're okay? Tell him he doesn't need to worry and say you won't be in for a couple of days because you have a lot to do.'

It felt odd and not really right for me to do it but I did. I held his hand in my left hand, and leaned on his chest with the right as I bent close and whispered. 'I'm going off now and I won't be back for a couple of days. I love you very much and I want you to know that the boys and I are okay. We're managing fine. There's nothing for you to worry about so you can just relax and sleep.' I gave him a kiss and left the room.

It was evening, about six o'clock I think. It took about twenty minutes for me to get home and as soon as I could, I opened a bottle of red wine, put my feet up and began to watch the television. It was a film, *The Shipping Forecast* I don't remember if it was a video or on the television. About half-an-hour later the phone rang. And you answered it. I can't remember the actual order of events but it was the hospital and I think they asked you if you were Mr Hartley's son, to which you naturally replied yes, and they told you he had died. I believe they thought they were phoning Geoff Hartley in Bucks because they hung up and rang again. This time you gave the phone to me. I wish I could remember exactly how it happened, but I can't. I only know that at that point I needed to get to the hospital quickly. I'd been drinking so I had to get a friend to drive me. Joe and Wills came too but you stayed at home. You knew he was gone and you didn't want to come with us. When we got there your dad had been gone for a while. I went alone into the single room he'd occupied for a few weeks. A white sheet covered him up to his chin and a small posy of flowers was on his chest. Joe and Wills went in one by one to see him and then we went home. I have a feeling that you felt guilty about not visiting him but let me tell you this: you were a good son, a patient loving son and you had to deal with a lot of stuff as a teenager. I remember once when your dad thought you were a stranger in the house. 'What's he doing here,' he asked us, 'is he another one of your boyfriends? He'd better get lost.'

'Don't worry Mum, he doesn't mean it,' you said and got up quietly from the table to walk away. It must have been really upsetting for you but you never made a fuss about it. The night he died you were only nineteen, and I suppose you might have felt that you should have behaved more like the head of the household; taken charge of things. But I never expected or wanted you to have that burden. I was quite capable of dealing with everything. I hope you didn't beat yourself up about it too much. We all muddled through, didn't we? Your dad died and things changed for us.

When I eventually got into bed that night I fell back on my pillows and my feelings at first were those of complete relief. I was thankful that your dad had been released from what must have been a time of torment for him. A weight had been lifted, but it wasn't long before I began to think about the man he had been for most of the time we were together. An intelligent, funny, clever man. I soon began to grieve for that wonderful person. Really, your dad died twice, once when the dementia took hold of his mind, and then when he left this world. It must have been so hard for you boys. But he was a terrific father before his mind began to lose things. He would have done anything for you. I am grateful that he didn't have to cope with your death. He had already lived through losing one child, Chris, when she died from cancer in her fifties. I now appreciate what a terrible thing it is to lose a child, and I think her death might have contributed to the start of his dementia. He was devastated. I know that he would have taken her place at the time if it had been possible. You don't expect your children to die before you whatever age they are.

Because of the virus that is gripping the world in its powerful and unpredictable jaws, we didn't manage to commemorate the tenth anniversary of your accident and death. We have been unable to meet up in groups, and shout our feelings of loss, love and hope. It has not been possible to honour your life in all the places you touched, from Buckinghamshire to Exmoor, Devon to France, Thailand to Australia, Italy, to Portugal and more. The 2021 Tosh tour did not happen. My second tattoo will have to wait, the family reunion in Italy will take place another year, the Gorf Jam will take place in 2022. All of this doesn't mean we didn't all celebrate in our own way because we did. Your little nieces talk about you all the time, not just on birthdays and anniversaries. They never stop asking questions. Evie, who likes to tell a joke or two recently asked, 'Were Uncle Tosh's jokes good?' Emily replied, 'Not particularly'. Which in itself is pretty funny. Evie wants to know what clothes you were wearing when you were put in the coffin, and I can't answer that question because of course, at the time, I couldn't look.

Time doesn't stand still and it doesn't do a lot of healing either. It is not possible to 'get over' the loss of a child and 'move on' as people are so fond of saying. I would suggest, from my own experience, that what happens is you learn to live with it. As the months and years roll on I can speculate as to what life would be like if you were still here. I can look at photographs and smile, but never without a little lump in my throat and tears are never far away.

It's all about learning how to grieve and accept that you're gone. I love that you stay close, and your memory is kept alive in this family. We talk about you all the time. We touch the few treasured belongings of yours that we have. We often cry for the loss of you. We want so much for your death not to have happened, but it has and we cannot change that. But what we can do is to keep you alive and with us in our hearts, every day in everything we do.

Love you and miss you Tosh.
Bye for now. I'll write again soon.
Mum xx

A DAY IN THE LIFE
Beatles Medley for Tosh

Hello goodbye   let it be
Yesterday you had all my loving
I don't know where you are
but eight days a week I'm crying

Yesterday you had all my loving
Perhaps it won't be long,
but eight days a week I'm crying
locked in a sad song

Perhaps it won't be long,
do you want to know a secret?
I'm locked in a sad song
the memories I can't separate

Do you want to know a secret?
Money can't buy me love. I know
the memories I can't separate
I feel fine   you're not here though

Money can't buy me love   I know
I get by with a little help from my friends
I feel fine   you're not here though
I imagine you to be at rainbow's end

I get by with a little help from my friends
but I don't know where you are
Did you ever find strawberry fields?
Hello goodbye   let it be

Before You Go...

A Note from Tosh's Sister

When Tosh died, it felt like he was everywhere and nowhere all at the same time. It still does. It was a shock to my system like no other, a Tosh shaped hole in the world far too big to ever fill. A grief that was all encompassing and came in waves. It still does. He is frozen in time for us now, always 27, always Tosh, always in our hearts.

I wasn't a parent when Tosh left us, but I am now. A big sister, and a mum of two girls. From the minute I became a mum losing a child became my worst fear and it's only now, that I can fully understand or even begin to conceive what a massive void he left in Mum's life. It has helped me to understand her as a person. She now expresses her honesty, vulnerability and true self in way she didn't before writing this memoir. I think it's been her therapy. In this book, my talented, unique and brave mother has shared her story. Our relationship has grown strong over the past ten years, but even stronger during the past eight; since I had children of my own.

This book is my mum's way of coming to terms with her grief. Though it's a memoir depicting the worst kind of loss, I love how uplifting and even amusing it is in parts, telling the important story of Tosh's short but wonderful life. A story he sadly didn't get to finish himself, but he would have been utterly thrilled to have seen what Mum has done. It's a truly amazing achievement, of which we are all so proud.

It's a gift to him, but also to us, Mum's other children, and anyone who reads it.

If only Tosh could read this book he would see how dearly he is loved and how deeply he is missed.

Emily

Acknowledgements

I would like to thank my husband, Geoff aka The Man. I can honestly say that without him, this book would not exist. Not only has he supported me emotionally and financially, he is my number one fan.

My gratitude goes to Laure, for allowing me to write this book for Tosh and for giving me permission to use her photograph of him on the back cover, and some of the beautiful words from her eulogy.

My wonderful children, all of them have helped by correcting me when my memory has let me down, or suggesting where I might need to think again before writing. Matthew, Emily, Joe and Wills who all lost a brother in 2011, have backed me all the way. Geoff's daughters Jackie and Lottie for their encouragement and help with PR.

Many thanks to Simon Banbury who allowed me a peek inside his precious friendship with Tosh. Also, Rhys Evans for writing to me with some details about Tosh and graffiti. Thanks Ronny (Oner), Tomo, Greg (Minto), Ross (Halo), Dan and Lew, for their unfailing support of the Gorf jam every year.

Cathy Rentzenbrink gave me so much guidance; backing my ideas for structure, and always ready to draw the very best from me as a writer.

My sincere thanks to my patient proofreader Frances Colville.

I must also thank my tutor Vesna Goldsworthy, whose comments on my first 5000 words of memoir, encouraged me to continue writing until I had a full-length book.

My fellow students from the MA creative writing course at Exeter University, in particular Carla, Gemma and Laura; they have been great sounding boards.

Thank you, Sarah Acton, and all the members of the Bridport/Exeter Poetry Stanza groups, for their feedback on some of the poems included in the book.

My writing buddies, Jane, Karen and Carolyn for keeping me going.

There are so many people to thank and I'm sure to have missed a few. But you know who you are. Relations, colleagues and my many friends.

Finally, Jpeg the dog. Without her I would not have walked every day through the vineyards of Languedoc, giving me the opportunity do so much thinking, remembering and creating.

Jpeg in France 2021

Ninette Hartley is a writer, mother, grandmother, wife and teacher. She has followed many paths – from acting and dancing to magazine publishing, and even driving a pony and trap – but she has always come back to storytelling. Ninette has an MA in creative writing and has been published in three short story collections. In 2015 she was shortlisted for the Fish Publishing Short Memoir Prize, and was longlisted for the Poetry Prize in 2020. She has won or been placed in several flash fiction competitions. After eight years living in rural Italy she moved to the Dorset countryside with her husband, Geoff, and beloved rescue dog, Jpeg. *Dear Tosh* is her first memoir.

Ninette in France Winter 2020/21